AN ENTREPRENEURS GUIDE TO MARKETING & SALES

CONVERTING CONTACTS TO CASH

MARY VIDARTE

TATE PUBLISHING
AND ENTERPRISES, LLC

Published by Tate Publishing & Enterprises, LLC
127 E. Trade Center Terrace | Mustang, Oklahoma 73064 USA
1.888.361.9473 | www.tatepublishing.com

Tate Publishing is committed to excellence in the publishing industry. The company reflects the philosophy established by the founders, based on Psalm 68:11,
"The Lord gave the word and great was the company of those who published it."

Book design copyright © 2015 by Tate Publishing, LLC. All rights reserved.
Cover design by Allen Jomoc
Interior design by Jimmy Sevilleno

Published in the United States of America
ISBN: 978-1-63418-114-3
Business & Economics / Entrepreneurship
14.11.06

To my loving son, John Andrew:
You are a heaven sent gift of love and encouragement.

GRATITUDE

Thanks to my dear son, John Andrew, for the endless hours of patience that you gave me while I interviewed countless customers, workers and business owners in every location we visited. Since the first day that you rode in the stroller, you have been my "little assistant", always by my side. Your cute smile could make anyone talk; all I had to do was ask the right questions. You continually provide me with an endless source of marketing and sales experiences.

Many thanks to Shellie Hunt, whose continued support guided me through moments when my focus was fading. Also much gratitude to Jim, John and Neil who have encouraged me to peruse my dreams and supported me in making it happen.

CONTENTS

FOREWORD

We are all entrepreneurs once inspired to see our gift or our calling to create. The creation of a business is like the birth of a child in that it is the accumulation of generations of learning. You will be offered the nearly spiritual opportunity to experience heavenly thrills of success as well as the hellish burning of failure. All of your life's experiences will come into play as you grow your business, just as with raising a child. If you don't presently own your own business (or are not a parent) you may be working for a company that an entrepreneur started. You may be participating as a corporate employee in an entrepreneur's creation, similar to the experience of babysitting. The corporate experiences may be a stepping-stone and training ground for your future business. How close you are to the that step may change as your role changes from a supportive role to a corporate leader or the creation of your own business. If not yet an entrepreneur, ask yourself, "What would I do if it were my business?" There are many ways to partner in the birth and growth of a business. For some, the partner selected may be a spouse or family member; for others, it may be someone who holds the greatest knowledge, skill set and common goals; or for others still, it may be as a corporate employee. Whatever your creative stage is in giving birth to your dream, there is something here for you. Your business is your baby, your heart, your soul, and your creation. Would you be risking all your time and resources for anything less valuable? Treat your business as you would your child. Stay connected and if you haven't connected with your children or loved ones recently, consider sharing the concepts in this book with the "CEO" of your home. You may be surprised at the correlations that surface.

There are many technical books about corporate marketing and sales, but small entrepreneurial businesses have unique challenges that need to be addressed. They are usually evolving with fewer resources and the CEO may be the only employee that is not an independent contractor! This book is designed to offer a systematic way of thinking, analyzing, creating and problem solving through a series of questions as it relates to the marketing and sales in a small entrepreneurial business. The dynamics of an organization are as unique as the type of business, goals, problems and solutions. By asking the right questions you will be better prepared to find your unique answers. The answers will change as the variables shift. This book doesn't give you the answers; it provides you with a process to find your own answers. Your way of running a business will be as unique as your parenting style is with your children. The end goal may be the same, but the process is your creation. Many of the questions are timeless and yet overlooked. As entrepreneurs, we not only work "outside the box" we also tend to work alone and ahead of the pack.

How many times have you thought, "If I only knew WHAT to ask, I could move closer to success?" Finding people who know more than you do that you trust, however, may be your greatest challenge. Once you find them, you need to know what to ask and how to filter the information. For those with more confidence and experience, the questions are internal and self-evaluated. As the basic questions are asked, more detailed questions unique to your business will emerge. It is the connections between the answers and the resulting actions that are chosen that will make the difference between success and failure. It's not just how you apply your IQ (intellectual intelligence) but also your EQ (emotional intelligence).

I designed the questions in this guide to be answered more than once and not all at once. It may be beneficial to let your subconscious mind work a while. Don't be surprised if the right connections between the answers appear when you are relaxed and least expect it to happen.

1

WHAT ARE THE HABITS OF SUCCESSFUL SALESPERSON?

"Since you were once a child, you were a salesperson many times and still can be."

The best salesperson I know is my seven-year-old. Since you were once a child, you were a salesperson many times and still can be. It's a matter of remembering the techniques from childhood. I learn about how effective selling happens every time my son wants something. Children have the unbelievable ability to figure out what it will take to get what they want quickly. With a smile, a grin, positive reinforcement, or if they don't get what they want, with negative reinforcement.

Somewhere along the way, some people forget how effective their childhood talents are. The best salespeople remember how to use their childhood selling skills as an adult. They remember how to identify who will respond to their appeal, what characteristics or approaches to use, for how long and in which way. They remember when enough is enough and when they haven't done quite enough. An effective salesperson remembers how to be fun, creative and interesting and sees selling as a game, just like a child. An effective salesperson knows how to stay aware of changes in the market and when to react on the changes in a manner that supports the customers' best interest, as well as their own. For example, a salesperson may bring a customer's attention to the need for a change due to an update in fashion or the introduction of a "better than before" product that will make their life easier or more wonderful. The effective salesperson understands that the consumers' need to stay fashionably current and socially acceptable are strong motivating factors that can influence a sale.

This is similar to how a child attempts to initiate change with his parents. An example of this was when my son, then five years old, placed a curtain rod on my keyboard while I was desperately trying to work and obviously not paying attention to him. He stated, "Mom, something happened in the play room" but really what he was saying was "Come play with me and by the way I don't know how the curtain got down by itself!" It was an event that forced me to stop what I was doing and react in order to proceed with my work. He designed a situation that forced a change and created a desired result that was in his favor. He was acting no differently than how effective salespeople sell. I realized that if I didn't respond to this "call to action" appropriately, a new approach would soon follow. Sure enough, in my son's case, the second "sales pitch" for attention included the use of sock puppets that started to invade my work space with "small" voices that repeated requests for attention. Just as in effective selling, flexibility, creativity, persistence and repetition are powerful techniques.

We have excellent examples of effective selling techniques demonstrated everyday in our own homes. We just need to remember what worked for us when we were children. What was it that you wanted so badly you were willing to pay a price for it? A bicycle? A doll? The latest electronic device? You were willing to do anything: a paper route, chores around the house, a lemon aid stand. Think of the attitude that you had at that moment in your life. Who did you sell your ideas to? What technique did you use? Did it work? How many times did it work? How many ways didn't it work? Did you stop? Why are you stopping now? Are you still using those techniques today, maybe in a more refined form?

You are a salesperson. How does it feel to sell "you" today? Possibly it was easier when you were a child. Maybe that's because it was the only way you knew how to get what you wanted. Today you have more options. If you don't like selling, you can hire or partner with someone to do the selling for you. Maybe you figured that out as a child and convinced one of your siblings to do all the hard work. That was an early childhood indication of your successful sales ability and in actuality, your first promotion from salesperson to sales manager.

Selling is what you make it, but to be the most effective, you need to believe in your product. If you believe in your product it is easy and can be fun! Not only do you need to believe in your product, you also have to stand behind your product with integrity. We sell from birth. We sell every day. As children, we sell our ideas and wishes to our parents. As adults we sell ideas and wishes to everyone around us. We sell ourselves. We sell our ideas. We convince others to see things in a better way. The first step is being aware that we know how to sell, then self-confidence comes with the fact that we recognize that we have been doing it all along. We also recognize where we have been successful and where we have not.

One of the simplest techniques to use while subconsciously or passively selling is to have something on hand that people are interested in talking about. Then it is much easier to start a conversation. Once the conversation has started the next step is selling your idea. An example of this is having a small child in a stroller while trying to make a merchandise return at a store. Everyone wants to stop and see your beautiful baby. This provides a diversion from the details or the item being returned and an attitude changing opportunity for the salesperson behind the counter. Things go much smoother if the salesperson is in a good mood, she thinks your baby is cute and that you are a nice person. You can even ask the salesperson to hold the baby. This is a technique of connection and relationship building. A few other examples of creative connection opportunities might be a single person going to the park with a dog on a leash attempting to attract the attention of other singles. They may let the dog do the work by attracting someone else's dog being walked by a single man or woman. Or the use of exotic cars that are often driven to attract new friends by creating an opportunity for attention and conversation. As successful salespeople, we have learned to combine the same elementary lessons that we used as children with more sophisticated "props" or techniques.

In addition to applying our childhood sales experiences, self-confidence is an important attribute in effective selling. Self-confidence comes not only through experience but also from feeling good about yourself and what you are doing. The more you sell, the more confidence you gain.

PERSONALITY TRAITS OF A SUCCESSFUL SALESPERSON

Think about the best salesperson you know. List the top five characteristics that you think make them the best at what they do.

1. _____

2. _____

3. _____

4. _____

5. _____

Think about the worst, most ineffective salesperson that you have encountered. List the top five characteristics that you think contributed to their ineffectiveness in sales.

1. _____

2. _____

3. _____

4. _____

5. _____

Here are a few of the traits that you should look for in a successful salesperson:

1. **Desire:** They should have a dominating passion to sell. Either they have it, or they don't.
2. **Motivation:** They will be motivated more by finding mutual benefits and closing a deal than anything else. We are all motivated differently. Usually this is based on our past experiences as well as our family values and childhood influences. Those who require management or outside motivation are less in control of their success. Therefore the more self-motivated a salesperson is, the more in control of their destiny and success they are. When interviewing salespeople it is always helpful to ask how they self motivate and manage stress in everyday situations as well as when in difficult work and personal situations.
3. **Awareness:** They will possess an awareness that they are good at selling and the end results reflect it. Successful salespeople know that they are good at what they do and they also know what it takes to be (and stay) at the top of their game. They have a special sense of self-awareness that guides them on each sales call, every day. Some salespeople will not make calls when they notice that they are not at the top of their game. Others say that going into the field and getting in front of custom-

ers brings them out of a low spot and back into a productive and positive state of mind. Awareness can be taught, but the most skilled salespeople have a natural talent for understanding how they are being perceived.

4. **Attitude:** They maintain an attitude that selling is not work, it's creative, productive, fun. We all have some reservations or resistance to approaching people and asking for business. For natural salespeople, the thrill of making the connection and talking about what they are selling is worth the effort, whether it results in a positive response or not. The natural salesperson sees it as an opportunity to meet a new friend. Even natural salespeople need training and practice to be the most effective possible, though. The training and practice is ongoing and expands in response to changes in the selling environment as well as changes to the products.

A common factor shared by many successful salespeople is an underlying positive personality. Always seeing the positive side of situations, they also choose to surround themselves with positive people. The most difficult situation is when your own family and close friends are the most negative people that you deal with on a daily basis. Family and friends provide a key part of a salespersons' stability, but family and friends also have the greatest ability to undermine ones positive attitude. The theories that similar personalities or energies attract each other appear to have merit when observing salespeople and their success. Positive salespeople have positive results; negative salespeople often show results that fall short of their goals.

One of my first sales experiences was an example of this. I was hired as a pharmaceutical sales representative with an elite division of one of the largest pharmaceutical companies in the world. We were formed as a separate sales and marketing division that was structured differently than any other company in the industry. Out of 200 salespeople, only 50 had no prior formal sales experience. Others in the industry said we would fail due to our horizontal structure and changes in how we did business that had never been accomplished before. A Harvard business study was conducted to track our progress.

We were a huge success and we changed the industry. Others concluded that the salespeople and staff that had the most difficult time adapting to the horizontal structure were some of the experienced managers and sales representatives from other pharmaceutical companies and those who had transferred over from the parent company. They were the most uncomfortable with the new structure and lacked confidence. The lack of confidence was not only in whether the goals could be accomplished, but also the basic concept that the job could be satisfying and enjoyable long term while simultaneously reaching and sustaining the sales goals. The employees that adapted the easiest were the 50 salespeople with no prior formal sales experience. They were also the salespeople with some of the highest sales results. I was one of those 50 people. As a company, we achieved our sales goals months ahead of our projected target, but, in order to effectively change the attitude of the experienced sales representatives and managers, professional leadership training was implemented as soon as the challenges were identified. As new salespeople, we didn't know that it couldn't be done. We were all overwhelmed with the huge learning curve and short time period given to become experts in three drug categories and sales techniques. We were so excited to have such a great opportunity; we never questioned whether it could be accomplished. We just kept pushing forward. It was a life-changing experience both personally and professionally.

Not every organization is suitable for a horizontal structure where communication and creativity is encouraged freely at all levels verses a more traditional and controlled vertical structure. Not all salespeople are suited for a horizontal structure either. Regardless of the structure, the attitude of the salespeople and management is critical to success. This is a clear example of what a positive work attitude and structure can accomplish as compared to a "less than positive" organization. It all starts with hiring positive people for the right positions.

Can you remember back as a child when having a positive attitude worked to your advantage? You knew you were going to win a prize or a game or do better than expected and you did? Can you think of a situation where as an adult you were the positive thinker in the group and your outcome was different than the others around you who were not positive about their expectations? A situation that you were confident was going to go your way when everyone else was not?

Look around you. Having a positive attitude has an effect on how people are willing to communicate with you and their openness. People can read your authenticity and they can feel if you understand them and, willing to accept them thereby making it is safe to share with you. This opens the door for a selling opportunity! Haven't we all met people that knocked at our door to sell us something and they were negative in their actions and/or their attitude? It didn't even have to be in their words, but the result was that you just wanted to get away from them. You were willing to even falsely say that you would buy something to get them to go away. What was your lasting impression about their product and company? Another example of how a positive attitude works best in sales.

5. **Discipline:** It has been said that even the best sales-people have to be disciplined. It's like getting up in the morning and brushing your teeth and getting dressed: if you don't you end up looking like a "bum". A sales-person must get up every day, walk out the door or pick up the phone, meet people and sell; or they become a "bum". Successful salespeople have the discipline to be in front of people every day. They also understand that discipline is necessary to keep their skills current, their mind sharp and their "selling spirit" alive.

6. **Self-Direction:** An effective salesperson must be self-motivated, patient and able to listen. You can teach people many skills but it is very difficult to teach someone to "want to work." It's a personality trait, possibly even a moral trait that is engrained in a person from childhood. Work ethic is key when hiring. They have to love it, want to be out there and not see it as work but as part of everyday life. They must be happier working and strive to be productive as a way of life. You can find a lot of people who want to work but they cannot self-motivate. They must be led or guided. Most true salespeople want to be free, out of the office or the box, making connections and closing deals. The thought of being in an office is stifling and seen as unproductive or a task for someone else to take on. You should be able to feel the energy when the right salesperson enters your

office. Once you have met the best salespeople, you will know the difference. The right salesperson for your company will give you the feeling that you should hand them the product immediately and let them walk out the door and start selling *today*! They are self-directed.

7. **Find the need and Fill It:** This is about the ability to connect the dots between clients, products, needs and opportunities. Not only can a true salesperson get out there and make things happen, they can see the connections between the opportunities with one client and opportunities with others. Salespeople are always making the connections because it's their natural way of thinking and seeing the world. Even though it may be a natural approach for them, training is still needed to identify the most effective ways to sort through the connections as it relates to products and clients. The more current and detailed your product and market knowledge is, the more effective the connections are. The best salespeople can imagine and connect the dots on a very small local scale as well as a broad national or international scale.

8. **People Person:** A people person has the ability, in a room full of people, to meet everyone while simultaneously ensuring that everyone is enjoying the process. Not only do they enjoy meeting people, but they do it in a way that does not over extend their visit or offend anyone. Some salespeople may close the deal, but may have also alienated someone in the process and limited their chances for repeat business.

9. **No Fear:** The most successful salespeople enjoy being out in front of people. In addition to being sociable, they also know how to control the need to talk to eve-

ryone and anyone. They have mastered the skill of focusing on what is relevant to closing a sale with targeted key clients and with the unexpected new client that may suddenly appear.

10. **Focus:** An experienced salesperson has the ability to remain focused and process various types of incoming data while targeting the decision maker at the best time. Sometimes selling is as easy as presenting your idea and asking the customer to buy. In many situations though, it can be much more complicated and require more advanced levels of product knowledge, communication skills and cultural awareness. The ability to focus on each issue at the right time and adapt your selling technique accordingly is the key to success. In order to have a higher level of focus, the sales information and message should be memorized and be first nature to the point of not having to think about it. It just flows. If you are unprepared with your product knowledge and presentation, it will be difficult to observe and respond to all the other important signs and messages happening around you.

Attention to detail is a helpful trait and habit. Many times it's the small details of what you observe that add up to an accurate picture. How many cars are in the parking lot? People in the lobby? Notices on the door or wall? Condition of the property or office? How are people dressed? What is the stress level in the office today?

11. **Flexibility:** Ability to be flexible with timing and sales techniques according to what the situation calls for. The most successful salespeople are flexible and know

how to change their routine and presentation quickly if the situation requires it. Less experienced salespeople will continue to give the same sales presentation even though it is obviously not appropriate or effective. They think it will be ok if they just keep pushing through, not using any discernment or objectivity. The talented salespeople are flexible enough to know when it would be beneficial to come back on a better day and move on to the next appointment.

12. **Connection:** The best salespeople can connect with all types of people from all walks of life in a sales motivating manner. If the products are uniquely sold to high-end customers or to certain ethnic or income levels, then the salesperson should become aware of what interests customers in those subsets. They understand the customer's interests and are able to converse and connect on things that they have in common. If there isn't any common interest, a skilled salesperson will develop a new interest in order to connect with the customer.

It is always helpful if you truly enjoy and understand the personal interests you pursue. People know when you are genuine. In some situations, it may be better to hire someone who naturally connects with the customer because they have similar backgrounds and interests. Selling, in many cases, is based on relationships. Unfortunately, shopping online has eliminated the relationship aspect of selling as we have known it, but there is always a customer who would rather talk to a live person than a website. The ability to connect with people online while selling is also a special talent that needs to be perfected. Even if the initial sale is not started online, follow-up and other customer service issues may be conducted with the customer online. The salesperson needs an awareness of what he has posted online and how it is understood by the consumer on the receiving end. Also, timing of how and when to send follow up emails is a learned skill. The truly talented salespeople know when to pick up the phone or get in the car and discuss things in person. Face-to-face connecting and communicating is critical in some situations. Even though technology has eliminated some personal contact in selling, we are all still human and we respond to personal interaction on a primal level.

13. **Communication:** Successful salespeople have the ability to communicate effectively with several types of people. Many people can connect with different types of people but lack the ability to communicate effectively enough to convey information and close a sale. Some situations require knowledge of different cultures and customs. Others require technical knowledge of the product being sold or of industry terms and procedures. All of this is in addition to basic language and presentation skills. Even a salesperson's local strong accent could prove to be a challenge for customers who are not familiar with the local dialect. In some cases, the local dialect could cause the salesperson to lose credibility with the customer. Then in other situations, depending on the industry and the corporate level of the selling, a salesperson with a strong local dialect or accent may have an advantage with local customers. The customer may consider the salesperson as "one of their own." The truly talented know what approach to take and when to take it.

14. Charisma: The best salespeole possess a personality that attracts people so that they want to stay in the salesperson's presence. Some salespeople are effective but not always pleasant to be around. Eventually, the less-than-pleasant approach may affect the close of new business or repeat sales.

When choosing the best approach, much depends on the industry, good judgment based on the facts of the situation and good timing. Some situations require a soft-selling approach. Others require a very direct approach. In some sales situations, selling is a social event requiring a more indirect approach. In situations that require a direct approach, the customer usually knows you are there to do business and appreciates the fact that his time is respected and that you quickly get to the point. Timing and reading the situation is critical. Life experiences as well as time in the sales field are advantages and are often reflected in salespersons' selling style and level of success.

15. Ambivert: Be an "ambivert." The most effective salespeople are not extreme introverts or extroverts, but actually those in the middle. They tend to listen better and know when to be quiet, when to push and when to hold steady. These skills can be improved through listening exercises.

2

WHO IS ON THE FRONT LINES?

*"Most importantly, we must sell ourselves
and believe in what we are selling."*

The first big question that most business owners and entrepreneurs ask themselves is, "Do I do the selling until I can afford to hire someone, or hire someone now?" Here are some mental steps to help you make the decision. If you aren't the right person, it could have a negative impact on your business.

Answer the following questions as they pertain to your work and hobbies to clarify if you should be doing the selling or not:

1. List the top three positive thoughts that you have about your ability and desire to do your own selling:

    a. _____

b. _____

c. _____

2. List the top three negative thoughts you have about your ability to do your own selling:

   a. _____
   b. _____
   c. _____

3. Which list was the least stressful to write and why?

   _____

   _____

   _____

4. List five current sources of marketing and sales information that you have recently referred to in order to keep your business knowledge current.

   a. _____
   b. _____
   c. _____
   d. _____
   e. _____

5. List five skills that you need to acquire or improve in order to be effective as your own salesperson.

   a. _____

b. _____

c. _____

d. _____

e. _____

6. List five work related tasks that you enjoy and do well.

   a. _____

   b. _____

   c. _____

   d. _____

   e. _____

7. List five work related tasks that you enjoy but do not do well.

   a. _____

   b. _____

   c. _____

   d. _____

   e. _____

8. List five work related tasks that you do not enjoy but do well.

   a. _____

   b. _____

   c. _____

d. _____

e. _____

9. List five work related tasks that you do not enjoy and do not do well.

    a. _____

    b. _____

    c. _____

    d. _____

    e. _____

Review and evaluate all the above lists. Now, ask yourself the following questions:

1. What tasks are you currently doing that you enjoy and do well and have appropriate skills?

    a. _____

    b. _____

    c. _____

2. What tasks are you currently doing that you do not enjoy, do not do well and lack appropriate skills?

    a. _____

    b. _____

    c. _____

3. What tasks would you enjoy and do well if you had appropriate skills and training?

    a. _____

    b. _____

    c. _____

4. What tasks will you never enjoy or do well regardless of skills and training?

    a. _____

    b. _____

    c. _____

5. What hobbies can you incorporate into your business to promote growth and success?

    a. _____

    b. _____

    c. _____

6. Compare your answers to question 3 above (list of things that you enjoy or would enjoy if properly trained) to the "Traits of Successful Salespeople" mentioned in Chapter 1. List the answers from question 3 that match the traits of successful salespeople.

    a. _____

    b. _____

    c. _____

d. _____

e. _____

7. Is your personality suited to the type of sales that you are involved in?

   Yes _____ No _____

8. If yes, list five things that you can do to increase your self-confidence about being your own salesperson?

   a. _____

   b. _____

   c. _____

   d. _____

   e. _____

9. If no, what other options do the answers to the above questions suggest that you focus on?

   a. _____

   b. _____

   c. _____

10. Is there a different type of sales that interest you that you would consider? If so, explain

    _____

    _____

    _____

11. If you are not a salesperson, can you hire or partner with someone who is?

Yes _____ No _____

So, what did you learn about yourself and your ability to be a salesperson? No matter how long you have been in sales and marketing, there is always something new to learn about yourself. Most importantly, we must sell ourselves and believe in what we are selling.

Many times, we are hesitant to hire or partner with someone who can fill in the gaps where we are not the experts or when we don't have enough time to do it all. This is probably because we have the misconception that we must do it all ourselves. Letting go of complete control over the details of running your organization may be contrary to the belief system that has made you successful up to this point. Your belief may be to control it all, all the time. Once you have accepted the fact that you may need to change your way of approaching the next level of success with your organization, you then need to decide how to go about it. Since this may be the first time that you have let go and delegated such a large task, clear steps may be helpful.

Control is not an easy emotion to face or let go of when it has driven most of your life. Your chances of success will increase by having a clear plan and a realistic understanding of the elements required. Those elements may consist of a detailed list of the tasks you are willing to delegate, hiring or partnering with the right person and clarifying the terms in a detailed contract. If any of these elements are poorly performed, delays in success may be experienced but usually can be corrected. If the right person is chosen, they can assist in identifying organizational goals and creating a more effective plan as well as creating a contract that ensures bilateral success. Hiring the right person may be the most important decision you make in guaranteeing the success of your business. Follow your instincts and you will know the right person when you meet them.

3

EVERY CEO IS AS GOOD AS THEIR TEAM

"Many skills can be taught but work ethics and personality traits probably will not change."

CHOOSING WHO YOU SURROUND YOURSELF WITH

This is an ongoing life-changing experience. Changes affect the very nature of our core security so many people avoid making them or even acknowledging that the people around them affect their success. The closer the relationship, the harder it is to separate from them, but the more we grow intellectually, financially and emotionally, the more imperative it is to have people around us, at home as well as in our organization, that are willing to grow with us.

Many skills can be taught, but work ethics and personality traits probably will not change. When hiring, ask yourself if the person being interviewed can grow with you and your organization. A different approach is needed if they can't grow with your organization over the long term. If you need their short-term skills and are unable to locate a better match in the given time frame, understand that it is a temporary solution and contract with the individual accordingly. Short-term contracts can always be renewed. Long-term arrangements are less flexible.

Focusing on team members with high EQ (emotional quotient) instead of just a high IQ may improve the quality of your team. For example, a high EQ person would show the ability to:

1. Correlate their behavior with the outcome of their actions

2. Evaluate the potential outcomes of their actions prior to engaging

3. Consider whether their actions will serve them well in the present time, near future and long term

4. Learn from previous experiences in order to improve their outcomes

5. Avoid ego-driven decisions

6. Be consciously aware of their intentions when interacting with others

7. Prefer accomplishing their goals without blame, manipulation, or dishonesty

8. Posses a win-win attitude towards life

High IQ, they know what to do. High EQ, they also think it through. Here are a few thoughts that a high EQ person may consider before taking action:

1. What is the goal?
2. What is currently being done to reach the goal?
3. Is the information on hand adequate to reach the goal?
4. After reviewing items 1 through 3, is there another approach to reaching the goal?
5. Are there other resources to help reach the goal?
6. What personal issues may be influencing my decisions that need to be taken into consideration?

KNOW YOUR BUSINESS

It is difficult to get the best answers about your business when you don't know enough about the industry to ask the right questions. If asked a question by a customer and you don't know the answer, it would be best to say that you will find out and retain their confidence and trust. Be honest with them. Once you know what things are relevant to your success, realistic goals and steps can be established to meet your objectives.

This is another reason to surround yourself with people who can bring knowledge to your organization. Can you think of a time when you were asked to perform a task that required the help of someone that knew more than you did? One of the easiest examples is probably a situation at home. As many of you know, managing your home is a lot like running a small business. If everyone doesn't do their job, stick to the budget and cooperate, things become much harder, unpleasant, costly and eventually could come to an end.

Did you ever need help the first time you did the laundry, or the second time after you had ruined the first load of clothes? Have you ever needed to ask for help when learning to care for a child? At that point, wasn't it an advantage to have people around you that knew more than you did? The same holds true in a sales organization. We all learn to put our pride aside and ask for help. In getting to know your business, ask for help from those who know more than you do. One day, it will be your turn to return the favor.

KNOW YOUR INDUSTRY

As your industry knowledge increases, so should your ability to apply that knowledge to how it affects your business. The ability to look back and analyze what has happened in your business compared to your industry and then observe your present situation will be key in determining your current status in the market. From there, the art of looking forward and projecting the action steps needed to meet your goals will be critical to accurately predicting your potential business growth.

In order to reach this stage of planning, you first must have a realistic and current assessment of your industry and where your business fits in. Some of the best ways to learn more about your industry are reading trade publications, researching online, attending industry-supported conventions, trade shows and trainings. Surround yourself with informed, knowledgeable people in your industry that you can learn from.

It is also possible to ask someone that you respect (either in your company or in another organization) to mentor/ coach you. There are ways of talking to the competition and learning more without giving out your business' competitive secretes. You may be surprised at how much they will share and how much you will learn. The ultimate experience is to work in the industry on a basic management or entry-level position long enough to understand what the priorities and hazards are.

KNOW THE PEOPLE YOU ARE SERVING

Once you know your business, it's time to learn about your clients, the people that you are serving. Due to economic changes, the people your company or industry were serving five years ago may be different today. Notice what those differences are and why the changes occurred. When there is a rapid economic change, it's important to make sure the information you are receiving about your business, industry and clients is current. It is reasonable to believe that your client base may continue to change as the economic market evolves.

4

MARKETING TO THE COMPETITION

"Be informed. Be the Buyer"

KNOW YOUR COMPETITION

Every industry has leaders and top industry is a small group. Go online and find out who your competition is and who the leaders are. At no other time in history has it been so easy to find out just about anything about everything in a flash of a second. For that reason, it is also important to remember what not to put on your website and let the salespeople of your organization give some facts out in person.

If you have thought of looking on your competitor's website, they have already looked at yours! The most valuable insights to your success may be those that you experience in person as a potential consumer. Be informed. Be the Buyer. Go out and look at the products. Do comparisons. Maybe even buy the competitors products and see what you think about the experience. You will know exactly what works and what doesn't work. You will know what features and benefits your product has that are superior to the competitions and which are inferior. You will also have time to prepare counter arguments against the competitor's strong benefits. This knowledge gives you the power to defend your product and anticipate what the buyer is thinking.

One of the quickest ways to figure out what is going on, other than being the buyer, is talking to the competition. The ability to filter what the competition says is imperative. The information they give to a stranger may be different than what they say to someone in the industry. Both types of information are important and you may learn more about your industry than you had anticipated. If you are new to the business, take steps to learn about your business before going in front of the established clients and new customers.

LEARNING FROM THE COMPETITION'S SUCCESSES

This is a task that savvy CEOs, investors, and those interviewing for jobs have perfected with the help of the Internet. Resources for obtaining new business knowledge include:

1. Company or manufacturer supplied information: Pamphlets, hard copy or online product descriptions of how to use, store, clean or return a product.

2. Online research: Searching the Internet by topic, key words, or phrases related to your industry.

3. Trade publications: Every industry has magazines or online publications and articles. This is a great way to remain current on industry issues.

4. Talk to salespeople already selling your products or competitor's products. Ask the right questions and then let them talk.

5. Talk to the store manager in the location your products or your competitor's products are sold. Find out what management's point of view is, compared to the salesperson's or the customer's. You may gain insight into why your product or competitors' product isn't preforming as expected.

6. Talk to your customers who are using your products or your competitor's products. The most valuable information will come from the consumer. The larger the opinion pool the more useful the data.

7. Be informed. Be the buyer. Pretend that you are the "buyer" and be a mystery shopper. Go to where your products and the competitor's products are being sold and observe, ask questions, take notes and evaluate the information. Consider buying the competitor's products or services.

8. Determine what your company vision statement is. The vision statement consists of inspiring words chosen to clearly and concisely convey the direction of the organization. By creating a clear vision statement, you can powerfully communicate your intentions and motivate your organization to realize a common vision of the future. Vision statements also define the organization's purpose in terms of values or guiding beliefs about how things should be

done (rather than bottom line measures). This offers employees direction about how they are expected to behave and inspires them to give their best. When the vision statement is shared with customers, it shapes their understanding of why they should do business with the organization.

9. Determine how you want the consumer to view your product and your company. Does your company's business model, business plan and vision statement support this image? Next, personally observe your salespeople and other employees to determine what type of image they are projecting. What image do they project on social media? Does the image of your employees match the desired company image? Keep in mind that the competition has probably already done this. How do your products, employees and company look through the consumers' eyes?

5

ACTION PLAN
MEETS RESULTS

"After assessing the future, the present and the past,
effective planning can be executed to ensure present
and future success."

PLANNING

Set goals and have an action plan to reach the goals. When the voice in the back of your mind says "you aren't going to meet your goals!", do you panic and get a plan and work or do you run and hide in another activity? We are all motivated differently just as we all respond to pressure differently. The personality of the salesperson should fit the action plan to reach the goals.

There may be more than one way to reach a goal. I have seen a variety of salespeople execute the same action plan in several different ways and still accomplish the same goal. Once the right goals are set, the next important step is to create an action plan to meet the goals.

To be successful long term you will need to constantly look in all 3 directions; in front, beside and behind you to get an accurate assessment of your business. After assessing the future, the present and the past, effective planning can be executed to ensure present and future success. Evaluate your team members in all three dimensions, too. Who is in front of you, such as, board of directors or investors, that is offering direction? Who is next to you that will assist in managing and directing? Who is behind you to implement and execute the details? The advantages of surrounding yourself with the right team members is explored further in Chapter 12.

GOALS

In order to set realistic, obtainable goals, you must first know your business. The more accurately you know your business, the more targeted and realistic your goals can be. Goals should be described with checkable, obtainable facts and completion dates. In addition, goals should be in line with the company vision statement and business plan.

There should be short-term goals and long-term goals. Determining the length of time for a short-term goal verses a long-term goal depends on the nature of your business, industry and desired end result. A short-term goal in the software industry, where things are constantly evolving, may be a month. A short-term goal in industries that have a slower rate of change and evolution, such as the food industry, or divinity may be a year. An easy rule to follow is that, short-term goals can be identified as those that are reachable within a year and long-term goals are those that will extend longer than a year.

1. List three short-term goals with projected completion dates that you have identified for your business.

   a. _____

   b. _____

   c. _____

2. List three long-term goals with projected completion dates that you have identified for your business.

   a. _____

   b. _____

   c. _____

REALISTIC VERSES UNREALISTIC GOALS

What are the differences between realistic and unrealistic goals? If you are new to the market and don't know what goals are realistic, refer to the same resources as listed under "Learning from the Competition's Success" in Chapter 4. It is an advantage to know the competition's goals and strategy. With some adjustments, you may be able to adapt some of the competition's goals and strategies as your own.

Knowing your industry and specific business is key in determining what is realistic. If you are weak in this area, it may be in your best interest to surround yourself with people who can fill in the knowledge gaps. Your idea of what is realistic is usually based on your experiences; those with more experience may be more aware of the differences between realistic and unrealistic goals.

Here are a few questions to ask when deciding if a goal is realistic:

1. Can this goal be accomplished in the projected time frame?

2. Does this goal fall in line with the company vision?

3. Is focusing on this goal going to affect the bottom line or just make me feel more productive?

Goals should be written down. When there are no written goals, it is more likely that you will obtain your subconscious goals. Usually subconscious goals are less focused than what could have been achieved had the goals been brought to the conscious level through written documentation. Once the goals are in written form, they can be more clearly evaluated, not just by yourself, but also by your whole team. Then, an action plan with measurements for accountability can be created.

Ideas have a greater tendency to become reality once they are in writing. Ask yourself if you are "settling for less" by resisting the work of writing down goals and a business plan. Why is there a resistance to these tasks? Is there a fear of accountability and the appearance of failure if written goals and business plans are not achieved? Is there a more productive viewpoint that should be considered?

WHAT IS THE DIFFERENCE BETWEEN CREATING GOALS AND CREATING AN ACTION/BUSINESS PLAN?

Action plans should be developed describing the steps needed to obtain the goals. To be effective, the plan requires review and updating constantly, even daily, as progress is made. The action plan may change frequently as more information is gathered and goals are reached. Most importantly, an effective action plan requires a measure of accountability that is recorded on a consistent basis. For example, if the goal is to sell eight widgets a day, the action plan might include:

1. Online daily sales-price advertisements targeted to current customers and known users of competitor products

2. Daily emailing to current customers and known users of competitor products by email to advise them of the sale

3. Phone call follow-up with emailed current customers and users of competitor products to remind them of the email and attempt to secure an immediate financial commitment resulting in a purchase

4. Daily sales results to be displayed on a scoreboard and updated each day at noon and closing time

An example of a company that did not have an effective business plan to deal with a changing industry is Kodak. They were forced into bankruptcy as digital photography took over the market and the use of film photography declined. They did not expand their product line fast enough to meet the changes in the industry, retain market share and stay in business. They were the foundation of photography and one of the innovators in their industry, but they will now be part of history instead of the present.

What are three examples of an effective action plan vs. a non-effective action plan?

a. _____

b. _____

c. _____

Some elements of an effective action/business plan are:

1. The action steps directly address the goal.

2. The action steps have a projected completion date.

3. Each action step has measureable criteria to determine if the goal is being reached. For example, the goal is to produce eight flawless widgets a day. A list of flaws and a team to look for flaws with their own criteria for accountability is established to ensure the goal is reached.

4. There is a scoreboard that all team members can see to tell if they are reaching the goal.

5. The scoreboard is updated every day or week as the status: information changes.

6. Each action step includes a backup plan for situations that have a predicable failure rate. For example, if historically three out of ten widgets produced in a day are defective, there needs to be an action plan with measureable steps to:

   a. Define a defective widget

b. Identify the cause of the defective widgets

c. Produce ten flawless widgets a day by reducing production of defective widgets

d. Correct, remarket, or dispose of the defective widgets

7. Incentive! Following the carrot at the end of the stick may work for farm pets, but highly motivated salespeople want to see the incentives. Is there an advantage to reaching the goal? Is there a financial bonus? A day off? A free trip? The clearer the line drawn from the goal to the action steps to the incentive, the greater the chances that the goal will be reached on time.

8. The team must believe that there is an achievable goal.

9. The team must believe that the action steps will get them to the goal.

10. The team must believe that they will receive the incentive.

EXAMPLES OF AN IN-EFFECTIVE ACTION/BUSINESS PLAN

1. No measurable data to determine if the goal has been reached

2. No scoreboard with obvious and understandable data reflecting current progress in reaching the goal

3. No specific steps describing how to carry out the action step

4. No date for projected completion of each action

5. No description of how accountability for reaching the steps and goals will be achieved

6. No backup plan to account for changes

AN EXAMPLE OF SUCCESSFUL PLANNING - SAM AND HIS VENDING MACHINE BUSINESS

Meeting Sam was an example of how easy it can be to learn about other peoples business just by asking! I met Sam in the parking lot of a warehouse superstore while he was loading his vending truck with merchandise. He had ten years of experience working part time as a vending machine distributor before leaving his full time job in healthcare customer service management. He has now been in the vending machine business an additional ten years. Sam has been very successful when others have gone out of business. He started his business in 2003 before the economic decline and believes that he has thrived while others have failed due to several factors:

1. He had a business plan and workable budget that both he and his wife were in agreement with.

2. He controlled his overhead and chose not to expand beyond what he could handle by himself without hiring any help.

3. He had prior knowledge of the business before leaving his corporate job.

4. He identified and acquired the best key accounts that would provide the bulk of his income.

5. He controlled his gas prices and vehicle expenses.

6. He paid attention to the market and understood what the situation would look like when it was time to sell the business.

7. He cultivated relationships with the potential buyers of his business as part of his exit strategy in his business plan.

Sam had plans to sell his business in six months to one of the suppliers of his vending products. He knew that the vending machines were going to change to more expensive electronic versions in the near future. Also, he was aware that the rules for placing those machines in public schools were projected to become much more limiting. The most economic products to sell in schools would be different types of water. The supplier for the water products controlled the pricing and the profits. They were the perfect buyer for his business. He formed a relationship with the beverage company. Three months later, he sold his business and its public school vending rights to the beverage company. Not only did Sam have a plan, he worked the plan and the plan worked for him. He was a success!

6

TARGETING, AIM, FIRE

"The most effective advertising and marketing will focus on the product's features and benefits."

TARGETING

Determining who your current buyer/end user is and who your potential new buyer/end user will be is one of the most important elements in maximizing your product's success. Once you decide what your target market is and what social-economic group your market is in; deciding what appeals to that group will be the key to closing the sale. Customers with less spending money may be motivated more by price and value than pride and ego. If they don't have a lot to spend, they will have to be convinced of the added value verses the risk of spending their money. Those with more spendable income may be more interested in the extras that appeal to pride and ego. Here is a list of targeting questions:

1. What are the features, benefits (advantages) and disadvantages of the product to the buyer? Many people do not know what a feature or benefit is but they know what an advantage is and they understand why it is an advantage. The most effective advertising and marketing will focus on the product's features and benefits.

2. Who are the current buyers/end users of the product? It is critical to understand who the buyers are in order to confirm other assumptions about product sales and buyer purchasing patterns. Also, knowledge of the customer's spending habits and needs provides another gauge for the budgeting of marketing dollars. The type of buyer determines how the product will be used.

   There may be a different general price range that buyers in specific market segments are willing to pay for the product than in other market segments. The better you understand the buyer, the more effective the marketing efforts will be in aiming directly at the desired group of end users. Knowing the buyer will also determine the length of time required to generate new customers or expand within the current customer base.

   Different types of advertising motivate different buyers. Having relevant information about your buyer's habits enables you to project the buyer's future needs as well as your future sales. Awareness of the buyer's future needs also enables you to gauge future product development in order to capture the desired segment of the market.

There is a difference between a white-collar and a blue-collar market, those who shop at Wal-Mart compared to those who shop at Neiman Marcus. For example, in the club stores, such as Sam's Club and Costco, products like organic olive oil or different cuts of meat may be sold in one of their stores rather than another and both stores may be located within a 15 mile distance from each other. Each location may have a different type of customer typically categorized based on income and ethnicity.

3. In what locations am I legally and logistically able to sell my product?

4. Who are the potential new buyers/end users of my product that will appreciate my products benefits (advantages)?

5. Where are the current buyers/end users located?

6. Where are the potential new buyers/end users located?

7. Is there more than one type of current buyer/end user for my product in each demographic area?

8. Is there more than one type of potential new buyer/end user for the product in each demographic area?

9. What type of marketing does the current buyer/end user of the product in each demographic area respond to best?

10. What type of marketing would the potential new buyer/end user of the product in each demographic area respond to best?

AIM

Now that you have targeted who you want to sell to, the next step is to choose the best method to aim directly towards them.

HOW TO GATHER MARKETING INFORMATION

List three sources of marketing information that would best influence your business.

1. _____

2. _____

3. _____

You may find that the amount of information you have gathered requires organization. An effective organizational system is needed in order to make the information useful. The key is to use a system that is most effective for you at the time. If you have limited computer skills and a limited budget, consider using paper and charts that make sense to you. When your budget allows for a more sophisticated method, choose the one that best fits your needs. Try to avoid taking on too many new critical tasks at the same time. Switching operating systems or updating software programs may not be a problem when setting up your marketing system if you are experienced in those areas, but if you don't have previous computer skills, avoid letting technology be the last stressor that sends you over the edge. Paper still works until you are able to expand your skills or hire someone to do it for you.

HOW TO ORGANIZE MARKETING INFORMATION

1. Start by gathering all the documents of current information that you have on hand.

2. Determine the physical location of your current and potential customers by using spread sheets, targeting software and/or marking on a physical paper map using different colored markers or pins.

3. Collect detailed customer information (into a spreadsheet, targeting software program, or a ring binder with lined paper pages) separated by zip codes, states, or countries.

4. Rank your current customers and projected new customers according to importance. Focus on a first tier and second tier sub group of customers, then select the customers you want to market to.

5. The final step is choosing the current and potential new buyers/end users that are desirable to expand market share and profitability with.

WHO TO TARGET

This is determined by comparing all the gathered information mentioned above with selected customers that have the following characteristics:

1. Resources to purchase

2. Need to purchase

3. Motivation to purchase

4. Most accessible

5. Require the most reasonable amount of company resources to pursue

HOW TO SELECT THE PRIMARY PRODUCT IN A MULTI-PRODUCT LINE

If you have more than one product, select the product that will offer a combination of opportunities: the greatest profit margin, the greatest market share, the easiest to sell and easiest to deliver. The actual number of products to focus on should be determined by the type of products being sold, the type of sales technique being used (phone, face to face, online, retail) and the company goals that are to be achieved. The targeting of primary products to focus on as well as the targeting of customers may change as more knowledge is gathered and changes within the market occur. Targeting objectives and conclusions should be reviewed frequently to determine if changes in strategy are needed. For a salesperson on the front line, a review may be needed after each sales call. For a sales manager, a review may be needed at the end of each reporting period, or more often depending on the experience level of his sales team. In the starting phase of any business, constant review may be needed. If targeting is inaccurate, it will be reflected in low sales volume and small market share.

7

HITTING THE TARGET

"Can you fit your product into one of the guaranteed established markets of birth, death, marriage, or divorce?"

Are you matching the peg with the hole when marketing? Why is hitting the target so important? You can do everything right, but if you miss the last step you will miss your target. The most successful salespeople are able to hit their target market effectively and efficiently using the least amount of work, materials and time. They know how to reduce the work of converting a call into a sale. Other salespeople may use different approaches and may get some sales, but time is money and knowing where to search for sales insures that you will maximize the your return on your time and resource investment.

Can you fit your product into one of the guaranteed established markets of birth, death, marriage or divorce? What are the buying habits of each category? How do those buying habits differ between age groups and locations? How does a consumer's age, with millions of people now over the age of 65, affect sales? What are their buying habits?

Age marketing is the process of separating marketing approaches and gathering information based on the age of the targeted consumer. Age is a major consideration in marketing; it is extremely important to positioning, merchandising and advertising. It is important to ask yourself, "What are the thought connections when a customer is making a decision to buy?" How do these differ between age groups, gender, income, ethnicity, and location? Understanding the uniqueness of the buyer for each product is the key to reaching that buyer with the right targeted marketing message and "pull" support. In merchandise marketing, the "pull" would be the process of moving a product from the shelf to the ultimate end user/consumer. The "push" would be the process of moving the product from the manufacturer to the retailer.

DIFFERENT LOCATIONS, DIFFERENT PRODUCTS BUT SAME CHAIN STORE

Multiple locations of a store will sell different products in different locations. Usually it is the demographics (the statistical characteristics of human populations based on age, income, gender, etc. that are used to identify market segments) which determine the product line and price point. Demographics may also determine the type, method and amount of discounting or clearance/closeout used to move products or reduce non-productive inventory.

You can learn a lot from the clearance section of a store, especially if they have multiple locations with different demographics. For example, in a grocery chain in the suburbs of Atlanta, it may be difficult to sell certain products that normally are purchased by people who do not have children. These items may be found in the clearance section in large quantities because the store misjudged their market. Conversely, if you visit the same grocery store closer to downtown with customers who have the same income level but very few children, the sale items may be different.

I recently experienced an example of this. I was amazed when I found a leading brand of organic rice and pasta on the clearance shelf at half price in the "have few children" side of town. I usually shop at the "have many children" side of town. Both sides of town have comparable income levels. It didn't appear to make any sense. After speaking to the store manager it became obvious that it wasn't because the "non children" people didn't like rice or appreciate the fact that it was organic. It was that they didn't cook as often because they have fewer children and they eat out! I remember the days when I did the same! I am sure many of us can reflect back to a time when our lives were simpler and our spendable income allowed us to eat out all the time instead of paying for the endless list of things our children need. The point is, the clearance section is where all the "targeting and marketing errors" go to free up profitable shelf space.

Another example is the dollar store. No one ever wants to see their life's creation of a best selling novel or biography show up in large quantities for a dollar. So, before you decide to create a great new product or write a book, go to the dollar store and take some time to skim through the failures to get an idea of what you don't want to do. Not all things at the dollar store are failures, but if the cover price was $19.95 and now it's selling for a dollar, something didn't work out as planned! Figuring out how to avoid being on the "best seller list" of the dollar store will be well worth your time. The problem may have been poor purchasing or marketing, not necessarily poor writing.

Many things need to go right to reach the customers who will pay the most for your products. I find it beneficial to shop in other areas of town to purchase items that have been on the market long enough for their marketing errors to catch up with them. Some sub markets will take longer for their marketing errors to show up on the clearance table because the buyers do not purchase the items as quickly or as frequently as they do in the major markets. Not only can you find some bargains, you will also find examples of marketing choices that you may not want to repeat in your business. Your perspective on bargain shopping will have a new meaning!

PRODUCTS CHANGE TO MEET CUSTOMER'S NEEDS

Have you noticed that long casual dresses were in style during this past summer season? This is an example of how products have changed to meet current customer needs. It once was that long dresses were only worn for formal occasions, but now as the majority of women in many age groups have increased in average size, so have their legs. Many women feel that their legs are less attractive than they once were, but they still want to look fashionable, comfortable and attractive at the same time. The long casual dresses made of cotton or easy-care fabrics are very popular and meet all these needs.

I noticed this trend in an average priced leading retail chain store. The price per dress was under $20; the colors were bright and cheerful, the styles were accommodating for small women as well as large. The true test of a marketing success is whether the customer buys it and wears it. It was obvious in the grocery store and the mall as well as on the beach that long casual dresses were a success. There were still plenty of very short summer dresses for those who wanted to show off their legs as well. A "well-targeted" competitor of this leading retail store also had similar long sundresses. The price was a few dollars more and the fabrics and style were slightly more upscale, but comparable. Both retailers responded to a need and the products were selling. The smartest entrepreneur will do the same by identifying the marketing opportunities and move on them quickly.

LESS SPECIALIZED PRODUCTS, BROADER RANGE OF BUYERS

The less specialized the product, the easier it may be to sell to the masses of people on a broader scale. The more specialized the product, the more targeted it needs to be. People care about the service that a product provides them. When the service is not obvious, the consumer will wonder what services the product offers them.

Convincing the buyer to make a purchase is more difficult unless you can make a complicated product appear to be simple. How can you make a complicated product appear simple? Draw a straight line from the customer's wants to what you are offering. Leave out the description of how it works. If the consumer wants more explanation, they will ask. If they ask, keep the explanation very simple. For example, the customer wants a fancy European sports car, but doesn't understand the engine and is worried about repairs. Point to your repair shop and the loaner car he can use if he needs to bring it in and remind him of the warranty that comes with the car. Sold.

Another example that is easy to relate to is how complicated it feels when faced with purchasing a new cell phone. How many of us truly understand our cell phone and it's many features? How much did you pay for your phone? How long can you exist comfortably without the use of your phone? Does it matter that we don't understand how all the features work? Have we all just accepted it for what it is? When making a cell phone purchase, do we just want the one that gives us the latest feature at the most reasonable cost? Yes! We have reached that point. We don't understand it all. We ask what questions are necessary and then we make a purchase! Remorsefully, in some instances, with a cell phone purchase agreement that last longer than many personal relationships do! If you are in doubt about making the purchase, a smart salesperson will suggest that you ask your child's opinion. Since kids appear to understand technological features quickly and know an opportunity when they see one, your child has probably already chosen at least 2 additional new items on the sales floor for you to purchased in addition to their new phone. Once your child has explained all the reasons to purchase (with more emotion and detail than the salesperson), you realize that you have been out numbered and purchase several more items than you anticipated. You still may not understand how they all work and you don't care, you just buy it all. Aren't children an excellent example of perfectly targeted potential buyers? They have intuitively figured out the details of closing the deal. After all, if it hadn't been for the mysterious accident that damaged your old, familiar, unattended phone so soon? would you have exchanged your phone? You would do almost anything to avoid all the complicated changes of purchasing a new phone. Was the mysteriously damaged phone really an accident, or an advanced sales technique set into play by your children?

This is an example of how a product that is very complicated to the majority of consumers is made less complicated. It's easier to "just buy it!" The benefits are obvious, the need is obvious and the salesperson makes it so easy!

LOCATION, INCOME LEVEL, PRODUCT

There is usually a correlation between income levels and where people live based on how much house they can afford. Usually, well-planned communities try to keep similar homes close to each other in similar price ranges. Keeping this in mind, there may be a correlation between where your targeted customers live, their income and their intellectual level. Typically, the higher the income, the higher the education level and the higher the price of the homes in the neighborhood. The clearer and more defined the demographics of an area, the easier it is to target areas of town that your customer lives in. Heavily populated, high-density areas are sometimes harder to separate into individual segments and may require more time in the field to sort out in person. If most of your business is online, the information needed for targeting will be different. With the changes in today's economy there are higher-educated people that may be working at lower-paying jobs and living in less-affluent neighborhoods. The question is, do they still purchase the same as they did when they had more income? So, it may be in your best interest to avoid making the obvious assumptions that we once did about income and intellect when discussing product positioning, price point, and value proposition.

8

PREPARE FOR SUCCESS

"When you are well-prepared, you can focus on the customer's body language and responses rather than checking your memory for product information."

PREPARATION

An essential key to success when giving a presentation about your product or services is preparation. You will know that you are ready to face your potential new customers when your sales presentation can be flawlessly given without any marketing materials on hand except the information in your mind. It is much easier to give a great presentation when you are passionate about what you are doing and it usually shows in the energy and feeling that the customer receives. The ability to verbally describe things so well that the customer can understand the point without having a marketing sales sheet placed in front of them is the true art of selling. The customer may not be able to repeat what you have said, but they understand it; they're sold on it; they want more. All this happens when you are prepared. Make sure you know as much about your customer as possible before meeting them.

PRESENTATION

The next step towards success is a great presentation. You must first know who your target market is so that you can determine the needs of the client that you will be presenting the service or product to. You may have more than one target market and therefore more than one presentation type. Ask yourself some clarifying questions. Who are you currently selling to? Why are they buying your product? Who is your competition? What is your customer's intellectual level of understanding your product? Once you have the basic facts, you are ready to create a sales presentation. There may be different lengths of presentations as well.

1. Very short – The "elevator" presentation that takes the same amount of time as a ride in an elevator

2. Short – A one to three minute introduction given when you first meet someone; that is longer than an "elevator" speech

3. Full presentation – A ten to fifteen minute discussion given when you have an appointment with a captive audience

4. A lecture – An hour presentation with a captive audience

You may want to choose a title for the presentation, and the right title for the presentation may not be obvious until after the presentation is completely organized. Organization time allows you the opportunity to think about the title while preparing it. Many people will get stuck on the title selection and never move forward to completing the body of the presentation.

When you don't know who your audience is in advance or if there is the chance that you may learn more about your audience that would change the level of intellect in which you present your information, be prepared with an alternate talk to address those possible variables. When giving a presentation to a large group, clarify whether the people asking questions in the audience are the decision makers that will purchase or use your product or service. Who in your audience is the decision maker? Are you holding the decision maker's interest during the presentation? The level of the questions presented will let you know just how much or how little the audience understands about your product.

The next step is to determine how many members of your audience understand at the same level as the person who is asking the questions. You may have one person who understands more than the rest and wants deeper details or you may have a person who understands less than the rest that needs more basic information. In either case, handling the situation so that you don't lose the interest of either group requires awareness and preparation. It is best to have a backup list of answers for situations in which there isn't enough time to go into a lot of details on either end of the discussion. Of course, a presentation with an individual person or a familiar group may be easier to prepare for than a large group or one you are less familiar with.

If you are involved in a live presentation and you are asked questions that you are not prepared to answer, consider asking the audience for their examples of a good response. Their perspective may be enlightening and offer the opportunity for deeper discussion on the topic. A few other solutions would be to refer to your website, offer to meet separately so that you can go into more details, or offer to have your assistant send more details after the presentation. One-on-one presentations are usually more effective unless you know the people involved and one member has already accepted or is favorable to your product and can help persuade the new potential customer to purchase as well.

You may have the option of using pre-prepared company or manufacturer provided sales materials instead of preparing your own. It requires less time and effort when you aren't "recreating the wheel." Many times, you can use the same sales material others have used and get a much more positive result. It is a matter of presentation and passion.

Practice out loud before you make calls by phone or in person. Nothing is more important than being prepared and well-schooled. Knowing the features and benefits (advantages) of your product and how they meet the needs of your client is imperative. You have to know your product, and the most effective way of preparing is to practice your sales presentation over and over until it is first nature. Say the words while you are in the shower, in the car or at the breakfast table. When you are well prepared, you can focus on the customer's body language and responses rather than checking your memory for product information.

First, choose one feature of your product that meets your customer's needs. Be prepared to explain the benefits of that feature. Then, connect the benefit of your product to the customer's need. When the timing is right, ask for the sale. If you have more than one or two products to present, evaluate the amount of time the customer is allowing you to have and adjust the number of different product discussions based on the time. You may be presenting too much information at one time. Select the product that is most likely to sell and choose the feature that is the most appealing to the market sector that you are presenting to. Keep in mind the length and the type of presentation should be determined by the situation that you are in. For example, in a social setting, the situation and the people entering the conversation may change at any time and require an adjustment in the sales approach.

Most customers respond best if the presentation is simple and to the point. Be prepared to expand on the information and answer questions about how the service or product is going to serve/help your customer. First, choose the sales technique, then the positioning. As you are listening to the client's needs, the positioning or approach to selling your product may change. Many highly successful salespeople create a short sales presentation and a longer presentation for each targeted group of current buyers/end users and potential new buyers. Knowing your competitor's selling points will allow you the opportunity to counter their claims, make the buyer aware of your product's advantages and encourage the buyer to purchase your product.

It is imperative to make sure all presentation information is accurate prior to releasing it publicly or presenting it personally. This enhances client trust. People want to know that you care about them, that they matter and their needs matter. The customer wants to be treated as though they are special, they want to be shown respect. They expect to be told when a product isn't right for them just as much as they expect to be told what, when and why to buy. In return, those that are already customers will come back as repeat customers and bring their colleagues, friends and family with them.

Choose the proper language for the presentation material according to the intellectual level of the audience. For example if you are speaking to doctors or lawyers that have a high level of education and more background information on the topic than the average person, more preparation may be needed in order to meet their expectations. If you are speaking to a less educated group and the presentation is too technical or the language is not familiar to them, the presentation will be ineffective and your sales goal may not be achieved. Knowing your audience is very important. It is best to have at least two different presentations for each intellectual group—a short three-minute presentation as well as a longer 10 or 15 minute presentation.

Keeping things simple is best, but simple when explaining a pharmaceutical product to a doctor will sound differently than explaining the advantages and features of the same product to the patient. The most important takeaway points should be stated within your first sentences. Then, explain in more detail as the presentation progresses and as questions are asked. Typically, it is easier to start with the basic "elevator speech" and expand from that point to the three-minute talk, then the 15-minute talk.

Here is an example of a typical dialogue when selling a prescription drug to a physician. "Good morning, doctor. I sell ABC product that lowers blood pressure faster than any other product on the market. May I leave you some product samples and ask that you consider starting at least three new hypertensive patients on ABC this week?" The three-minute discussion may mention the same information but expand by including facts about how "ABC not only has the quickest onset of effect but also controls blood pressure smoothly and consistently for hours due to its once-a-day dosing. ABC's once-a-day dosing also offers an advantage to the patient of less uncomfortable side effects by avoiding the rise and fall of blood pressure, which is commonly experienced when taking a shorter-acting drug." And of course, the longer discussion would answer questions the doctor would have about the product.

The same can be done for any product and any audience. It is easier to start with a short version and then expand to the longer version. Asking the customer questions concerning the products they currently use will keep them engaged in the conversation, offer you more information about your competitors and insure that you are addressing the customer's concerns. Asking your customers questions is also one of the easiest ways to determine your selling approach. The customer will lead you straight to their areas of concern so that you can address them and make a sale by meeting their needs. Some other questions could be: Why are you using those products? What features do you like the most? What features do you like the least?

KNOWLEDGE

Understanding your product, industry and competition is imperative and your knowledge needs to be current.

Reading published articles concerning successful competitor's product sales, advertisements and websites is a good way to stay current in your field of expertise. Also, searching the Internet with industry-related words, phrases, or new market problems could give you a competitive advantage. This allows you to not only see your competitor's pitfalls but also mimic their successes. Each product and industry has different knowledge and information demands.

You need to know your buyer and their product needs better than they do and be prepared and ready with solutions to meet their needs. A successful company knows that products may need to change to meet their current and future customer's needs. The company's ability to make the changes is dependent upon their ability to look ahead and predict the customer's need. Then, the company's ability to provide a solution is dependent upon innovation and ability to collect new information.

The final step is to adapt all that is gathered to form new products. An effective way of constantly keeping up to date with both changing needs as well as available solutions is to read and search daily for information concerning your industry. Do your homework. Be prepared to answer questions about current events related to your product or services.

ROUTING

Know where you are going, who you are going to meet and how to get there before you get in your car. Get on the phone or the Internet before you make a sales call.

1. Use current targeting data to create a routing system that allows you to contact your most important customers in person, by phone, or email.

2. Use industry specific routing software or a self created system which includes a GPS and a ring binder of targeting information set up by zip code, county, state, or country.

3. Create routing schedules to access the first and second most important groups of buyers and current users first.

4. Select days and times that will achieve the highest probability of generating business.

5. Call key buyers/end users to determine the best time to see them in advance of creating your routing schedule.

6. Stay on a schedule so the buyer/end user will be expecting your visit the same time each week or month.

7. Determine how often you need to see a buyer/end user and schedule it in advance.

APPEARANCE

Your first appearance and first impression leaves a lasting imprint in the consumer's mind about your brand and your industry as a whole. A bad first impression may lead the customer to believe that you are not worthy of their business and they will tell others the same. An adverse first impression may also have a cumulative effect. This refers to relatability. You need to be able to relate to those you are selling to. Most of all, the customer has to feel that they can relate to you.

The buyer may feel that you can't relate to their industry and to their needs if your appearance isn't what they are expecting. For example, what if you are selling farm equipment to a farmer and show up in a suite, or you are going to a board meeting and show up in farming work clothes? The impression may not gain the customers confidence. Dress as though you matter and feel you deserve to be there. Be appropriate for the situation. You represent your brand, your company, and your industry. Ask yourself, "Do I look as though I belong in my industry?" Check to make sure that your clothing, grooming and style are current and appropriate for your age. If you are not sure, ask a salesperson in a retail store that you respect and that understands your audience. Let them know what you are trying to accomplish. Practice being the buyer. Will the salesperson give you an honest answer? If you don't feel as though you received an honest answer, ask more than one person in different locations. One of the most effective resources may be someone that is successful in your industry.

COMMUNICATE

Communicate effectively, clearly and appropriately. The key to being a great salesperson is the ability to communicate. If the customer doesn't understand your targeted message, they may not buy your product or service! If the human element wasn't needed or desired by the customer, they would just buy everything online. Although many things are purchased online, customers are human and usually want to talk to a human in most situations. It is important to be more effective than your website by adding the "in person" warmth of a smile and tone of voice that reaches another level with the customer and encourages a sale the way no website can. In other words, you have to bring the human element of face-to-face communication to the forefront. The customer will have an additional perspective to base his decision on that the website doesn't offer. The customer gains the ability to feel personally understood, connected, safe and valued. Therefore, what you say and how you say it makes a difference. For example, everything may be going well until an improper tense of a word or the wrong words are used and then the client loses respect and/or confidence. Keep in mind that confidence for your customer is imperative when they are considering a purchase or repeat purchase.

Know the difference between communicating in a "white-collar" environment and a "blue-collar" environment. Be aware of current terminology used by the level of employees that you are addressing. One of the most economical and beneficial resources may be to join a speaker's organization in your local area. Keep in mind that not all speakers groups are created equal and the quality of the advice given is only as effective as the success level of those giving it. What is considered an "A" talk in a small town may not be up to standards in a large metropolitan area with an audience of highly educated listeners.

TIMING

Timing is everything. Be aware of what is happening around you when making a sales call. Determine in advance the best time to contact the buyer. Be in front of the buyer regularly and at the same time of day and same day of the week if possible. Then you will become part of their anticipated daily routine. Your message will be remembered better if it's anticipated, regular and frequent. Be aware of the personality and habits of the person you are speaking to. Notice their body language and adjust your approach, language and timing of words and speech appropriately to accommodate their changing body language. Examples of body language may include how a person is standing, facial expression, direction of vision, or the tone and speed of their voice. If you become aware of body language, it will be easier to connect with the customer.

CONNECTING

Know how to connect with each type of buyer/end user for each type of product or service. Make connections between events, other products, opportunities and conversations. These new connections may offer the opportunity to present your products in another way to new or present buyers. Be genuine; the client knows the difference. Be honest. A buyer is more likely to do business with someone that they can connect with versus someone they cannot. Look for common ground and topics that you can each relate to. People like to be with people that are similar to them

9

MARKETING: STAND OUT IN THE CROWD

"What was once the desire for self-serving items is now the desire for self-freeing services and products supported by competent customer service."

STAND OUT IN THE CROWD

The reason you want to stand out in the crowd is so your products and services are not confused with the competition. If you want to stand out, there are several things that you can do. For example, location still matters and customer service is in high demand. It's not just your product that can stand out; it's also your service. It's a proven fact that even if you may have a "me too" product (a product that is similar to others on the market) with little or no tangible point of difference, the exceptional service that is provided with the product may win you top market share. This may hold true even if your product costs more than your competitor's. People will spend more for a product that better meets their needs, which include excellent customer service.

Today there is a need for customer service that equates to reliability and a feeling of security. The old rules of marketing in the 1940s and 1950s were geared towards mass marketing. The focus was status and self-worth. For example, a woman's self-worth was greater if she had a washing machine. It was viewed as if her time had more value therefore her status was raised. Every woman deserved to have a washing machine.

The new rules of marketing include the idea that customer service is now a customer-engagement strategy. In other words, the customer wants to see how the solutions will assist them in solving their problems or meeting their needs. The customer has to feel engaged and part of the process. The customer wants more than just the product; they want service to go with the product. The ability to keep up with the changing social masses and marketing appeal is a skill that separates the average from the best in marketing and sales. Another change is the movement from once being a "me" society to now being a "we" society. In other words, in the past, the best marketing approach was to appeal to a buyer's ego, convincing them that they deserved to "have it all" and "have it all" at once. Now that we have had it all, all at once, as a society we are realizing the most valued commodity is our time. We have become slaves to the things that "own us" rather than us owning the things. We want things that make our lives easier and less burdened. We want it all but also we want to be free from the burdens. We want a relationship with the product manufacturer or retailer that offers service if something goes wrong. We want a sense of security that goes with each purchase. What was once the desire for self-serving items is now the desire for self-freeing services and products supported by competent customer service. It's all about service, freedom and liberty. Today, we all have washing machines and modern appliances, but now we want the Internet screen on the refrigerator with a place to keep a shopping list and online ordering of kitchen items. This is in addition to a pop-up message to tell us when the appliance needs service with an automatic message going to the appliance repairperson. The additional services that go with products make people feel as though they matter. If you can convince someone that your product will make his or her life easier, you are one step closer to closing the sale.

LOCATION

Some things still remain true in business: Location, location, location! There was a time when "location" meant where the real estate was located and this was held as being a factor that would never change. Today, location is still important, not just as it relates to the location of your store, but also your location on the sales floor shelf and on the Internet. If the sale of your products or services require the buyers or clients to come into your location, they must be able to find you before you can make the sale.

Have you ever been told about a great sale at a new store and after searching for 30 minutes you gave up trying to find the shop? Even with a GPS, it can still be hard to find some places. The lack of visibility from the main road and not being able to access the location easily are big obstacles to overcome. Making the right location selection in the beginning is one of the most critical decisions. It is usually best to hire an experienced realtor who specializes in the type of location you are looking for. A qualified real estate broker can provide research on available locations as well as information on where your competition is located. Depending on your industry, you may or may not want to be located near your competition. The best locations are usually more expensive than the less desirable locations, but in some instances a less desirable location may be great for a business. For example, as a retail shop you may not want a location on a street that is around a corner with limited street visibility even though it offers double the private area parking and easy access from the back of the parking lot. Your customers may not be able to find you. But a retailer who needs room for all his established motorcycle customers to park and test ride motorcycles may love it! A retail or office space that is located on a street with limited visibility, obviously built in a below-ground-level hole next to a noisy train track or smelly trash dump will probably not improve over time. If you were the consumer, would you be able to find this place? And if you did find the place, would you go inside? Put yourself in the customer's shoes and see what your decisions would be.

SAFETY

Safety is another issue. Some locations may be safe during office hours but rather scary at night. Your customers may not be visiting at those hours but are your employees working late? Will you or your employees feel unsafe after hours? Will you have problems with store security or property insurance because of crime? A qualified real estate broker can assist you in acquiring details needed to make these decisions, but ultimately they want to make a sale and the depth of the information may be influenced by that fact. It is best to verify the facts by doing some of your own research on crime and zoning. Always go to the location and observe it during all hours of the day and night before making a final decision.

It is, always best to verify what road construction and development is expected in the immediate area. For example, have you ever been blocked from accessing the gas station that you have been using for years because of a sudden broken pipe or road construction? Then, after a week you realize that the construction isn't going to end for another two weeks? By the time the construction was completed, you found a new gas station to service your needs. Not only did the gas station lose business for several weeks, now the regular customers were in the habit of shopping someplace else. Some retail establishments cannot survive several weeks of reduced sales.

As a real estate broker and a business broker, I saw this happen many times. Very successful businesses failed because of changes that occurred in the accessibility to their location that were out of their control. Sometimes a sudden change such as a broken pipe under a road is not controllable, but many times the changes were public knowledge, possibly in the planning stages, and it was up to the tenant or purchaser to be aware of them. One example that I was aware of involved retail land and strip malls at a very busy intersection in a high growth area across the street from a popular outlet mall. Many tenants and buyers new to the area were not aware of the proposed overpass that had been approved to pass over the busy intersection. The landlords and sellers of the property were very much aware of the proposed changes and leveraged their knowledge effectively. This would leave the current high-visibility locations below the overpass with distant entrances and exit ramps diverting traffic away from their stores and office fronts. Not only did this affect traffic flow to the businesses, it also affected the purchase and lease prices of the locations. Many tenants were locked into long-term contracts with stiff penalties for breaking their leases or had purchased the property at high prices. The decrease in business due to the overpass construction alone would be more than many businesses would be able to survive.

THE INTERNET

Not all products and services are sold from stationary buildings or locations. The Internet has changed how we sell, but your location on the Internet is just as important as where your store or kiosk is located on the street or in the mall. The Internet presents a new marketing paradigm that requires a new action plan with new marketing rules. The position of your storefront is stationary, but your position on the web changes with activity. For example, if you want to discover what your Internet presence is, simply conduct a web search of your name and company name and see what comes up. What you see is what the customer and your competition will see. Making changes to your image isn't difficult, but hiring an expert to help build and position your website and web advertising may be an advantage. You may want to check your site and conduct a web search of your name each week to see what things have changed. You can no longer overlook the Internet as being vital to your business.

SIGNAGE

Signage is also an important factor. Have you ever been out searching for a location and there was no sign, or the sign was not visible? Did you eventually find the location and go in or did you just give up? We have all just given up at some point. One of my first businesses was a muffler franchise located on a very busy road near customers with cars and money and an average amount of similar competition. The delay in zoning for a street sign almost killed the business. The details were all in the agreement when the building was built. No amount of planning can compensate for the politics involved in dealing with zoning when you don't know how the inside system works. Eventually, a sign on wheels was placed near the street. Every day, the zoning inspector would come and measure how far the sign was from the street and threaten us with fines if we didn't comply. Every day there was a new objection and every day we moved the sign. Finally, we put the sign in the back of a pickup truck and parked it in the parking lot near the street until our permanent sign was approved and the sign marque had been completed. I am sure many of you have become more familiar with your local zoning officials than you had ever planned to be. How many of you have seen signs that totally missed the mark so badly that it made you laugh?

Do you live in an area that has unique ethnic areas where all the signs are in a different language such as

Chinese, Korean, or Spanish? Many metropolitan areas have these types of communities. If you go into the stores you may notice that even the product labeling is in a different language and the salespeople are not speaking English. Somewhere in the translation something went terribly wrong with the signage when the English version was posted below the Spanish or Chinese. The lesson to remember is, if it's not your first language, get a professional to do the translation.

Conversely, how many of you have seen great signage and billboards that really hit the spot? So well that you can still remember them now. One of my first memories of effective signage was traveling from North Carolina to South Carolina and seeing "South of the Border" billboards. By the time you had seen what seemed like 100 billboards for the last hour or two of driving, you had no choice but to stop and see what "South of the Border" was all about. If you had kids in the car, it was impossible to pass up such an adventure. How about the Chick-fil-A billboards with cows trying to get you to eat more chicken? What a brilliant idea. And as you probably know, one of the first signs a child learns to recognize is the McDonalds golden arch, not always to eat the food but to play on the playground!

If you are in doubt about how your sign should look, pretend you are the customer and ask yourself, "Can I read the sign easily? Is the sign clearly representing the store so that I can tell what is being sold? Does the sign entice me to go inside to shop? Is the sign compliant with zoning and codes so I won't have to pay to have it remade?" Looking into what the zoning and the landlord will allow for signage should be done before making a decision to lease or purchase a location. If you can't advertise your name effectively, a different location may be a better choice.

KNOW WHO YOU ARE MARKETING TO

Before you can identify who you are marketing to, you must first understand your product's features and benefits. Your product may have more than one market or application. If you are marketing to upscale customers with higher incomes, you may use different marketing approaches as compared to customers in a lower income bracket that may have a different application for the product. Getting the input of a carefully selected focus group or hiring a marketing research team to determine your target market may be beneficial. If your development budget is limited, form your own focus group of carefully selected people who will give unbiased opinions. Observe what your competition is doing and who they are targeting. A lot can be learned from what has already been done.

Go shopping and pretend that you are the buyer. Compare similar products to yours. Have you ever been shopping and found a product that was so dysfunctional that you wondered if there had been any test marketing? Or was it just a manufacturing problem that went terribly unnoticed? I have personally seen several products of this nature at the stores that cost you only a dollar per item. Once you understand your product's attributes, features and benefits, you can more accurately determine what market segment to target and what approach to use.

HOW THE BUYER MAKES DECISIONS

After determining who the buyer will be, determine how that particular buyer makes decisions in your industry. In your business, is it the lower income buyer who is more concerned with price and quantity than fashion and labels? Or is it the higher income buyer that isn't as concerned with price but must look unique and fashionable? What is the price point in which each group will decide to buy? What price point is too high and will cause the buyer not to make the purchase? Are there factors that will encourage the buyer to overlook these limits and spend more?

CONNECTIONS BETWEEN PRODUCTS AND OPPORTUNITIES

When "you know what you know" in your industry to be right, don't let others change your mind or influence your hands-on expertise. Nonetheless, to be on the safe side, figure out why they think they are right and see if there are any flaws in their logic or in yours. Always verify your knowledge and your personal feelings to make sure you are clear and not motivated by underlying personal issues that may interfere with good business judgment. Listen to others who are the experts; check their facts with what you already know. Look deeper. Use what's already there in the market. You don't have to have an original product, maybe just a variation of any existing product.

When creating something new, first look at what's working and what's not working in the market.

List three experts in your field of business whose opinion you trust concerning marketing in your industry.

1. _____

2. _____

3. _____

List three products already in your market that you could improve on and sell.

1. _____

2. _____

3. _____

Notice what's missing in the market. Don't recreate the wheel. If there is part of something that is working, use the idea and modify what's already there.

List three products that are missing in your market that present a need and a potential opportunity.

1. _____

2. _____

3. _____

Know the competition. Always be aware of the prices, features and benefits of many different types of similar products. Then, you will be better prepared to identify a good product at a great price when you see it. Also, follow how different products perform to learn from what works and what doesn't work. Look at pricing, size, color, and packaging. Notice both their similarities as well as their differences.

List three products in your industry to follow as indicators of how to position your products. List why you have chosen them to be your benchmarks.

1. _____

2. _____

3. _____

Mystery shopping is a wonderful way to learn firsthand what is happening at the customer level in your product category. It is a technique that you can hire others to do or do it yourself. It involves going into the market place and shopping for your products and your competitor's products. You are pretending to be the buyer. You are gathering pricing information. You will notice how your product is positioned on the shelf. How your packaging compares to others. You can watch other buyers and see how they react. Ask the buyers questions just as if you didn't know anything about the products but wanted their opinion. People usually love to talk. You may notice how the buyers in Wal-Mart view your products differently than the ones in Target. And if you haven't taken your product to market yet, what a great way to figure out what is currently working and what isn't working. You should consider purchasing and using your products as well as competitive products in order to complete your product and market evaluation. This technique takes all the mystery out of it!

List three locations that mystery shopping would be effective for your products.

1. _____

2. _____

3. _____

10

MARKETING RESULTS

"Your product's complexity and your understanding of the market should determine the approach chosen to track your progress"

Once the wheels of success finally start turning, a system of checks and balances will be needed to determine if your goals are being met. Your product's complexity and your understanding of the market should determine the approach chosen to track your progress. As you learn more about all the variables involved in gaining market share, you may find it necessary to make changes in how you track your success. The smallest amount of sales and marketing information may change everything. The easiest way to track information about the market share of your product and the industry is by keeping records of your past and current sales. Keeping detailed notes on each change that occurs with your product is very important. Your data is only as good as the details. This includes online as well as in-store sales. Examples of the types of information that may change your marketing approach are current trends or current material levels available to produce your products. It is important to have a clear understanding about who your target market is and verify that the target is being reached in a timely and effective way.

List three specific early indicators that will determine that your target market is being reached in a timely and effective fashion.

1. _____

2. _____

3. _____

List three specific intermediate indicators that will determine that your target market is timely and effectively being reached.

1. _____

2. _____

3. _____

List three specific late indicators that will determine that your target market is timely and effectively being reached.

1. _____

2. _____

3. _____

Determining how to capture the sales of an untapped market when you have a "me too" product and the competition has the market share requires a creative strategy. As mentioned earlier, a "me too" product is one that is similar to others in the market place with very few marketable differences from the competition. One example of a creative strategy is to add a service to your product, such as free delivery, that instantly offers a marketable point of difference. This is a way to make a win out of a difficult challenge, even if the volume of sales gained amounts to a relatively small market share. In short, nothing is "left on the table." The question is, can you take the relatively small portion of market share and grow it into a larger part of your business?

Notice how major retailers expand and control their market share. When selecting products and locations, they analyze a significant amount of research and demographic data in order to capture niche opportunities. Use their knowledge and expand on it to meet your needs.

Remember though, just because big retailers have done it doesn't mean they will succeed, or that what they have done is a good approach for your business. You may not have the resources that they did to make it successful. A big retailers' success may actually have been a failure had they not put as much money behind it to correct their hidden mistakes. Keep in mind that the more time it takes to reach your goals, the more resources it takes to sustain the company until the profits are generated. Where a large retailer may have as much as two years of reserved resources to support their marketing efforts, you may only have six months to turn a profit before you are out of business.

Who are the leading retailers in your industry targeting? Is that your target market? For example, if you are a small grocery store in the food industry, which large grocery chains accept EBT (Electronic Benefit Transfer) or SNAP (Supplemental Nutrition Assistance Program)?

Which accept WIC (Supplemental Nutrition Program for Women Infants and Children) benefits? What requirements do they have to meet to participate in these government programs? Are these programs important to your clients? Is it worth the cost and effort to offer these options to your customers? Are the products that you offer on the list of acceptable items for purchase under the programs?

Out of the big chains that take EBT, SNAP, or WIC, which ones are most familiar with processing the purchases for EBT, SNAP and WIC customers? How easy is it for the customer? What part of town are they located in? Is their target your target? Many large chains will honor EBT, SNAP and WIC because they are required to in all their locations but have very few customers that use the services at certain locations because of their demographics and income levels. In other words, the EBT, SNAP and WIC customers can't afford to live in certain areas of town so they don't shop in those stores. Even high-end organic grocery store chains honor EBT and SNAP purchases. In other words, just because you see the EBT, SNAP, or WIC sign on the front door does not mean it's a clear indication of that retailer's target market. Talking to the store manager is always helpful. They know what goes on in their stores. This is also an example of when putting yourself in the customer's shoes could provide you with very valuable information. It's always good to experience being the buyer.

11

HOW CAN YOU HOLD YOURSELF ACCOUNTABLE?

"Holding yourself accountable is a process of choosing a technique to implement an accountability 'checklist'"

ACCOUNTABILITY

We all have our own personal patterns that have made us successful in our planning and executing of tasks. The challenging step may be in identifying what techniques work for yourself and what techniques work best for holding your staff accountable. What works for you may not be the best technique for those who are of a different personality type or in a different job. There are volumes of books written on how to inspire others and ourselves. The art is in figuring out what works for whom and when it works best. It is generally an accepted concept that accountability is necessary for long-term success. For many entrepreneurs, however, it may be difficult to decide on the guidelines of self-accountability while constantly monitoring their evolving business and evaluating what realistic expectations should be. In large corporations with highly structured environments, many of the goals and execution steps are clearly defined in order to increase productivity and accountability. In either environment, holding yourself accountable is a process of choosing a technique to implement an accountability "checklist". In situations where the path to success may not be as clear, here are a few key points that may help clarify your focus.

1. Be honest with yourself about the facts of the business. How many of your decisions are based on something other than the business facts? Sometimes we can be our own worst enemy by holding on to ideas that may be driven more out of ego than by good business sense.

2. Have a board of advisors. If you are stuck and can't think of solutions or can't hold yourself accountable, know when to ask for help. This requires having a support group or advisors that understand you and your business and have your best interest in mind.

3. Have a written strategy plan with indicators for critical anticipated changes. Compile a list of events that would trigger the next critical change in your business and describe what the indicators will be in order to determine the best time for change. For example, when to expand your inventory, when to hire more workers or when to move to a larger

location. Follow your indicators and hold yourself accountable so that the best decisions will be made.

4. Keep accurate records of sales, buyer/end user details and competition.

5. Evaluate your data regularly. In some situations, a daily review of every call every day is needed so that you can make changes in your strategy and daily interaction with clients. In other cases it may be a monthly review to determine the next month's approach, or an annual review to adjust long-term goals and strategies. Compare your data with your business and marketing plans to see if you are reaching the goals.

6. Have a current business plan with obtainable goals and plans of execution with end dates.

7. Report and review sales and marketing information regularly. Requiring progress records in the form of a weekly report is the first step, even if the report is primarily made for yourself. Next, require it from your employees and subcontractors. Once it's in writing it is easier to track and focus on the goals.

8. Review targeting after each sales call and know when to say "next" and not look back.

9. Stay focused on today and let go of what happened yesterday.

10. Follow up. Make sure products and services are delivered as promised. Delivering "excellence that exceeds the expectation" is a very powerful differentiator between your value proposition and the competition.

11. Know the basic details about your products. This will improve customer service and enable you to be more efficient and effective. It is important to realize that some salespeople have to be taught to think ahead and to anticipate obstacles. It may not be their normal way of thinking. In that case it would be beneficial to identify this training opportunity very early and either effectively train them or put them in a different position that doesn't require the ability to anticipate a customer's needs. The change in the salesperson's interaction with the customers should be noticed immediately once they are taught what to do. It may take time to learn the basic facts about the products but a general awareness of customer needs should be immediate. The salesperson can learn to let the customers know that they are new and that they need a few extra minutes to gather the information. Customers usually understand and will be patient.

12. Know the key clarifying questions to ask yourself and others in order to determine if you are reaching your goals. Know what to ask, when to ask and who to ask.

13. Accountability in selling requires lead time. Make sure that your salespeople are fully prepared in advance to professionally meet the customer. In other words, think the whole sales process through and allow enough time for all the detailed preparations. Implement an effective review system that includes accountability checkpoints to reach the lead-time requirements and achieve the ultimate goals.

12

WHAT ARE YOUR ASSETS?

"The people you surround yourself with can be your greatest asset and resource towards success"

Do you know what your assets are and who you need on your team to succeed? Who takes care of your accounting? Who takes care of your daily "red tape" problems that every business experiences? Who makes your sales materials and keeps up with the sales contacts and contracts? Who will you need on your team to make your business grow in a year or two years? If you are always looking ahead towards what you will need next to grow the business, you can create a plan to get there. The people you surround yourself with can be your greatest asset and resource towards success.

Who are your team members? Look in three directions and assess your situation. Who is standing next to you? Who is standing beside you? Who is in front of you on the organizational chart? Choose wisely where you want to stand and who you want standing next to you. Are those you have chosen trying to move up the same ladder you are? How will they handle competition? Determine how you may be treated and be prepared with an action plan in the event that they choose to bring you along as a team member or if they choose to leave you behind. Are they honest? What are their ambitions? Are they "yes" people? Whether you are the boss, a partner, or a co-worker, surrounding yourself with people who know more or who have more wisdom than you in an area of business or life can be a valuable asset. It will, however, require maturity and self-confidence on your part to allow it to happen.

A challenging situation is when you mature enough to notice that the people that surround you are not as positive an influence and don't necessarily support you or your business' best interest, especially if the non-supportive people are also part of your personal support group such as your family and close friends. You then can decide if you will ask for more support, choose to create more distance from them, or simply recognize the situation and continue as before with few changes. Who you choose and what situations you choose to accept will affect how you succeed.

Who are the leaders in your organization? You may want to look ahead of yourself at those who have more experience. They can be a valuable resource, but choose wisely. Age doesn't always indicate relevant experience or guarantee a path to final success, nor does youth always indicate innovation and creativity. You will know who is right for your organization when you meet them. The more people you interview, the clearer the solution and choices will be. So, always have an open eye for talent. Your competition will be looking for the same type of person and you may want to get to them first.

When do you become the leader? Many times we become leaders when situations demand it—in good times of increased sales or conversely, in difficult times of declining business and problems. It helps to have people lead that want to lead. Most of us have been leaders in areas that we don't think about, at home, parenting, or in social activities with our extended families and friends. In the work place, it is similar but with the added dimension of profit and loss, hiring and firing.

Who are your followers? Look behind you. How do you feel about how they are conducting themselves and their business? What is the correlation between what you see and what you think your image is projecting that they are modeling after? The personality traits of a successful leader include:

1. Visionary – Successful leaders have foresight and imagination to see creatively outside the present confines. They can envision achievable, larger goals prior to their existence.

2. Communication skills – The ability to effectively communicate with others from different generations, viewpoints and backgrounds in a collaborative way is definitely an indication of a good leader.

3. Accountability – A successful leader will possess a willingness to accept responsibility for their actions or lack of actions.

4. Integrity – This refers to the adherence to a code of moral or artistic values with honesty and truthfulness.

5. Inspiring – A great leader supports people in tapping into their self-motivation to feel good about achieving their end results.

6. Ambition – Successful leaders have the ability to achieve personal and company goals.

7. Patience – Good leaders can remain steadfast despite opposition, difficulty, or adversity.

8. Humility – The ability to be humble and not project pride or arrogance so productive learning can take place, is an important mark of a great leader.

9. Courage – Successful leaders are able to do difficult things and to over come fear.

The real test of leadership is how a leader/CEO will react when things don't go according to plan. CEOs need to be adaptable and the plan has to have flexibility when things shift. It's not "if" the unplanned will happen, it's "when" it will happen. In life as well as business, things don't always go as planned.

What less desirable situations could you avoid bringing to your businesses if, as the leader, you change something that you are currently doing? Since you are the common leadership denominator between all the aspects of your business, do you see any correlating factors between your leadership decisions and business events that you can improve on? Your past experiences will determine your unique perspective on running your business, whether this is your first experience in the less structured world of self-employment or if you have never had a structured corporate job. If you find that you are lacking in one area, consider surrounding yourself with those who have the skills and experiences that you are lacking.

13

SUCCESSFUL JOINT VENTURES AND PARTNERSHIPS

"High IQ means they know what to do.
High EQ means, they may or may not know,
but they will think it through"

When evaluating who you will choose as a partner in business, it may be beneficial to have an idea of what their IQ (intellectual intelligence or apparent relative intelligence) and their EQ (emotional intelligence) are. Watching how they respond in certain areas of decision making will give you indications of how they may respond in a business situation. An easy way to remember what IQ and EQ stand for is in the form of a rhyme: *High IQ means they know what to do. High EQ means, they may or may not know, but they will think it through.* EQ is better defined as emotional maturity that is reflected in the ability or desire to correlate personal behavior with personal outcomes. If executed correctly, the ability to evaluate the outcome of your behavior should expose advantages that will serve you well in the present time as well as the near future and long term. This ability usually requires identifying and separating oneself from decisions that are driven by ego instead of sound business facts. The ability to learn from previous experiences in order to improve your current and future condition is a learned art. It is possible to assume that a person with a low IQ may not be able to solve problems or learn new tasks as effectively as a worker with a higher IQ. In essence, a more mature employee may make more effective decisions than the smartest, less mature employee. The added dimension of what each workers EQ is, will determine how effective their decisions are. In the structured corporate environment, there are systems in place to guide those who may not have the experience necessary to make the best decisions, but in a small business there may be fewer checks and balances in place to identify and isolate poor decision making before the consequences are too great to recover from. For this reason, it is very important to choose your partners, investors and workers wisely.

KNOW BUSINESS OWNERS AND ENTREPRENEURS MINDSET

Entrepreneurs are a unique group of people. They operate and are motivated differently that other workers. They are risk takers, dreamers and visionaries. But first generation entrepreneurs are not always motivated or view things the same as the second or subsequent generations in a family owned and operated business. Many corporations start as small family businesses and many entrepreneurs view their business as their family. Understanding what the thought process is for each influential member of a company is important in gauging the cooperation you will receive when implementing an approved business plan or changes in general. For example, a family member that has grown up watching his parents create their dream may have the expectation that it will all be left to them once the parents step down. When the heirs realize that the business has passed its prime and no longer viable and won't be their parachute, they find themselves without a workable plan for the future. They feel as though they have been mis-led and now stranded. The outlook by the heirs is greatly determined by how they were brought up in the business. Did they work at all levels of the business or did they just receive the rewards? How will they transition if a parent passes suddenly or if a parent chooses to sell the business for large profits and the heirs are left with no identity associated with the business? Some family members have little or no interest in the business as long as they continue to receive the financial benefits of the business. Other business family members are intimately associated with the business as part of their identity and have never envisioned themselves without the family business. Separating from the business would have been comparable to losing a child. Many business owners have become so distraught by losing or selling their business that their mental and physical health was affected by the transition. These are very important topics to approach when setting up exit strategies and partnering with small business owners over long periods. What is their plan? Do they have a plan? Are all the family members aware of what the plan means if a sale or loss of the business were to occur? Do they understand that it is "BUSINESS"? For many, the business is a creation and a part of their soul. The family members may have a very difficult time fitting into a different business model, even if that includes an increase in revenues that ultimately makes them a big success. How will they handle success? Is this the first generation of success for this family? Will they exemplify "New Money" behavior? If they experience failure, will they take ownership for the losses or will they blame you and others? Even with a plan for success, failure and an exit in place, once implementation occurs, you may see behavior that is not conducive to reaching your goals due to the emotions that become involved in the decisions. Self-sabotage may become an issue.

List three examples of situations in which not understanding the thought process of a family business owner resulted in a negative effect on your business or someone else's business dealings with them.

1. _____

2. _____

3. _____

KNOW YOUR BUSINESS PARTNERS' OTHER BUSINESSES

Many entrepreneurs simultaneously have more than one business venture as a strategy to offset unexpected losses and create alternative income streams. It is in your best interest to understand what businesses and industries your partners and investors are involved in, and what priority each one has in their cash flow strategy. If a dramatic change occurs in one of their other businesses, whether it is an increase in profits or a decrease in profits, there may be a change in how they view their investment with your company and how much risk they want to take. It is in your best interest to be aware of how your partner's other investments are performing on a regular basis. You need to be able to assess the situation to better determine how your partners will make decisions with your business if they have a cash flow problem.

Even if you are legally and financially sheltered from the other businesses, the effects of losing the support and knowledge of a partner that is involved in daily details of your business could be detrimental. The partner's trust, knowledge and support may not be easily replaced in the short term or the long term. Your goal should be to know as many important facts as possible in order to determine your risk and create a strategy in the event that the worst situation occurs.

How you decide on acquiring this information should be determined by the relationship that you have with your partner. For example, let's say a partner's primary income is earned from an established chicken farm of which he is the primary owner. There is a chicken virus or bacteria outbreak requiring the extermination of all the chickens. Is your partner insured for such a loss? How long will it take before the insurance company will pay? Can your partner survive the wait? What if there isn't any insurance? Who will they turn to?

If your partner's main source of income is a travel agency and the economy takes a downward turn resulting in fewer travelers, how would this affect his cash flow? If the there is a major national disaster effecting a large metropolitan area of the US and your partner is in the military reserve or National Guard, what are the chances that he will be called to serve? How long will he be gone? Who will have the authority to make decisions on his behalf during his absence? How does this affect your business?

Your managing partner wins the lottery. How does this affect your business? Is he coming in to work again? A year from now, could he have tax problems that could extend over to your business assets?

KNOW YOUR BUSINESS PARTNERS FAMILIES

A partnership in business, whether it is short term, long term and regardless of how it is structured, is like a marriage. What happens in the partner's personal life may have a significant effect on your business. You may choose not to investigate completely or you may need the partner's support and the partner may not be willing to offer all the information. You need to know what the questions are so you can plan ahead and weigh your risks. The more you know and properly evaluate, the better you can assess your risk. For many things, you can use common sense and determine by observing how they live and whom they spend time with. Let's look at a few examples.

A partner may get a divorce and his wife may have claim to part of your company. How many divorces have they each already had? Do they appear to be a stable couple? Do they show examples of respect and effective communication between themselves and other family members?

What is the trust level between the family members? Always meet the spouse and family if possible. If the kids are reckless and poorly organized, they probably learned it from the parents. What outside family members control what happens within the family? How will those relationships influence your partner's decisions about the business?

A partner or one of his dependents may have a drug or alcohol problem; they may have undesirable involvement with the law that could involve your business if they are driving a company vehicle on company time or on company property when the illegal acts occur. Also, if one of their dependents or spouse is involved with the law, their illegal acts could have consequences for your business. If federal laws are involved for example, (i.e., drug trafficking, tax evasion, or money laundering), your company assets could be seized in an investigation merely by association. It is important to do a thorough background check on each partner to make sure you are insulated from unnecessary risk. Once you have secured the information of concern, legal advice may also be advised. If your company is viewed as having deep pockets (lots of assets), you are more likely to become a target for those who want to file suits. Remember, most people do not understand the true finances of having your own business and that cash flow may be very low much of the time. The average person is under the impression that an entrepreneur or small business owner has plenty of money to pay for lawsuits (unless of course it is someone that you want to borrow money from, and then they think you have no assets or potential to earn!).

A partner may have illegal workers in their home or in one of their other businesses. Smart lawyers will find ways to pierce the corporate veil of separation between businesses and personal affairs/assets to get to other pockets of money. Check it out. Better to know what your risks are ahead of time (even if you choose to partner with someone who is a high risk), than to find out what your risk is on the six o'clock news!

What if a partner lives financially beyond their means? What have their long-term spending habits been? When the partner's money runs out, where are they going to go to get money? After investigating the partner's finances, how long before they go broke? What are the consequences to your business if they go bankrupt?

A partner may be forced into bankruptcy personally and/or under one or more of their other businesses. What are the consequences to your business if this occurs? At least if you know ahead of time, you can write the proper agreements and structure your partnership so that the damages are limited. Bankruptcy provides protection and relief so that personal and corporate assets can be protected. Does your partner have a moral issue with filing for bankruptcy if needed as part of your corporate asset protection strategy? You need to ask. You may be surprised at what some very well-educated business people will say. If they are not willing to take that step corporately to preserve assets in a crisis, you may want to reconsider the type of partnership you form with them. They could jeopardize your ability to protect your share of the assets. They may be willing to consider a bankruptcy, but what is the influence from other family members? You need to understand the family politics.

Let's say a partner has excessive student loan obligations for himself or his family members. Most student loans are not dischargeable in bankruptcy and will continue to influence your partner's financial decisions. If leins are placed on your partners' assets, how will it affect your business? Does he plan to use his assets as collateral in the partnership?

Here is another example: A partner or his family members have a risky lifestyle that could result in sudden unexpected medical or legal bills. Most entrepreneurs are self-insured or have health insurance through a spouse's employer. If the spouse loses their job or one of the other businesses is no longer able to support the cost of health insurance premiums, the partner will be in need of money. How will this financial need influence the partner's ability to operate objectively as your business partner? A few examples of risky behaviors are: excessive drinking, smoking, obvious signs of poor health and engaging in high-risk sexual activity. Or, does your partner participate in activities that insurance companies identify as high risk, such as skydiving? Many executives keep their health issues confidential to prevent investors from becoming nervous about who will be making decisions about their investment in the event that the worst thing happens. "Key Man" insurance is also an asset that investors like to see in place.

A partner's public image could negatively affect your business. For example, your partner is seen on the news expressing a politically/socially incorrect point of view or arrested for a serious crime. How will that affect your business? You may still choose to take their investment money and/or allow them to function in the day-to-day details of the business, but you will need to have a plan of how to handle difficult situations if they occur before your business suffers the consequences.

A partner has other unrelated business partners with high-risk life styles and businesses that could affect your partner personally and/or legally. For example, your partner may be involved with partners who have illegal businesses or are involved in the buying, selling, or manufacturing of less proven or less stable products in unstable markets. If your partner checks out clean but his other business partners are high risk, what happens to your business if your partner is taken down for his other unrelated business partners? It is similar to practicing safe sex; you need to make sure you are protected legally and financially from all the other partners that your partner may be "in bed" with. You may still choose to "sleep" together, but be aware of what the danger signs are and have a plan of what to do about the situation if things take a turn for the worse. It is always best to know the source and unspoken terms of your investment money and favors.

KNOW HOW JOINT VENTURES AND PARTNERSHIPS OPERATE

The most important first step in structuring your company is to consider good legal and financial advise. The structure of your company should be determined by several factors, such as tax implications, type of business, projected income, nature of your investors/stock holders, etc. Once you are comfortable with your knowledge concerning the type of structure you want for your business, you may find that some types of corporations can be established online by yourself for a limited cost.

Whatever corporate structure a company may be under, all successful strategists and CEOs create exit plans with the sale of the business in mind. The goal is to build the most profitable business that reflects the highest business value possible. Planning for and creating the highest business value positions the business for the best possible sale. Buyouts are almost always an option. Many business owners see their businesses as their "babies," or their creations similar to that of a child that they have given birth to. Some owners are happy to sell and can't wait to retire. Others experience challenges in finding a new identity and purpose in life after the sale of their business. Details may be written in purchase/buyout agreements to preserve the nature and identity of your business, but that doesn't guarantee that it will be honored even if you will be continuing on as an employee of the company for a limited transitional time. Those who specialize in acquiring small businesses understand how important these details are to making the deal and will include them in the contract. But they also know the price of what it will cost the seller to defend their position if the buyer decides to change the company image and violate the contract. For some sellers, the fact that they received their money in the bank on time is all they care about. For others, no amount of money is truly enough to replace their lifes creation. In the end, the best sales price is the one that both sides agree to.

14

HOW DO YOU PROTECT YOUR INTELLECTUAL PROPERTY?

*"Your most valuable asset may be your clients
and your greatest liability may be keeping
their information secure."*

Intellectual property (IP) is an idea, invention, or process that derives from the work of an individual's mind or intellect. Intellectual property includes industrial property such as patents, inventions, trademarks, industrial designs and geographical indications. In addition, IP includes copyrights such as poems, novels, plays, films, music, drawings, paintings, photographs, sculptures and architectural designs. Intellectual property is also your company information, employee information and your client's information that you have a responsibility to keep secure. If your competition gained access to your customer list and contact information, how would it affect your business? Protecting your company information isn't enough. Your client's information must also be protected and clients expect their identities to be safe.

Your most valuable asset may be your clients and your greatest liability may be keeping their information secure. Protecting client information is a growing concern for small businesses as well as large corporations. It may be in your best interest to hire a professional to evaluate the security of your clients' information. Keep in mind that your teenager that can "hack into anything" or your office manager that set up your book keeping are not the professionals that you need. Most theft occurs from within the organization by present or past employees that have or gain access to data. Many times a "data breach" that results in the loss of a client's information is covered by insurance, but often the policyholder is denied payment for the loss due to a lack of compliance with specific rules written in a policy designed to keep data secure. For example, how many people can access secure company data from a personal device that is not password protected? Is your cyber insurance policy void because passwords are not being used on all the devices of users that have access to secure company data? Are you prepared for the legal action that clients can take against you if their data is stolen from your company? The consequences of not keeping your clients' information secure could cost you your business.

If your product or service has unique market advantages, having patent or trademark protection is probably in your best interest. In addition to data, patent and trademark protection, you can purchase insurance to protect your business in the event that your patents are infringed upon, or if you infringe upon the patents and trademarks of others. Be sure to read the fine print, as not all policies are created equal. In all these situations, the advice of an intellectual property attorney and an insurance expert in IP coverage would be advised.

Has a patent attorney specializing in your product market assisted you in applying for your patents or trademarks? Did you do it yourself? Where were the patents and trademarks filed, domestically in the US or internationally? Do you have the minimum amount of resources to defend your intellectual property if challenged? Is it part of your budget and do your investors understand why these funds are needed? Many very smart entrepreneurs spend a lifetime developing their dream only to have it stolen. The greater your intellectual property's impact is on a market, the harder the competition will work to get it for free. Many entrepreneurs are aware of what they have to gain if they are successful but overlook the consequences of what the competition will face and what the extent of competitions efforts will be to protect their market share.

It is not uncommon for a large industry-controlling corporation to partner with a small entrepreneurial company to help bring the entrepreneur's product to market. Even with the most sophisticated contracts in place, the more powerful, dominating corporation may attempt to gain possession of the IP. They may invest enough time and money to learn everything needed about the IP then file a cease and desist order claiming there were violations in the contract between them and the entrepreneur. Ultimately the owner of the intellectual property is not allowed to do business. The goal of the dominating corporation is control. The IP may remain in the entrepreneur's possession but restricted from being used in that industry or market. Restricting the intellectual property's use may prevent or delay industry-changing technology from entering the market and therefore perserve the dominating corporation's market share. Usually, the dominating corporation will know exactly what your assets are, how long you can afford to defend yourself, and who all the judges and attorneys are in the jurisdiction of the violation. You may not be their first victim. Doing research before signing any contracts may be in your best interest.

An important step is filing your patents internationally to avoid being cornered in the local courts where the large corporations have unbalanced influence and control. Once the corporation is aware of where your patents are filed and what your resources are to defend ownership, they then know what, when and how to acquire your IP most effectively. Even in more honorable situations, a weaker position on your part equates to a more favorable acquisition on theirs. They have control and you cannot out spend them or out influence them in a legal environment that they influence by the nature of their power. Filing your patents internationally cost more but may offer more protection against local leverage.

The dominating corporations usually want to keep you in their comfort area of control, which usually is in their "back yard." Even if you have internationally filed patents and trademarks, the contracts you sign may require that you agree to handle all disputes in the corporation's local jurisdiction. It may be the price of doing business. Sometimes the best option is to sell your IP and move on to the next adventure rather than holding out for perceived larger returns. For many entrepreneurs, however, their creation is their identity and it is difficult to let go.

Were you working at a corporation when you designed your IP? Read your employment contracts. Many companies have complete rights and control over anything you develop or work on while under their employment. They may not be required to pay you anything for your creations, not even royalties, even if you have patented/trade marked it, and even if it is in an unrelated field. The closer the correlation is between what you did for the employer and the products you developed, the stronger their case in acquiring your IP. It is best to have an attorney address these issues prior to employment if the products are already developed or are being developed.

Whose name is the IP registered to? Under an individual or a corporation? How is the corporation structured? You need to get legal advice on how to structure the ownership to maximize the protection of your asset. A corporation considering a partnership with you to bring your product to market will probably have already checked out all these details prior to any consideration. They will know everything about you, your family, your associations and your weaknesses. Ask around and look around. What other entrepreneurs and their products have they attempted to work with before you? Contact them and ask questions. You may be surprised at what you learn. If they received any compensation for their IP, they may be under contract and not allowed to answer any questions concerning the situation, but you will get a feel for what is going on. You should always be aware of what and who has preceded you. What was the net effect? You may pay for legal advice, but if patent defense isn't the attorney's expertise, you may have wasted your money. Your real estate attorney may be cheaper and a good tennis player, but it may cost you your life's dream.

Patents and trademarks of your own are important in order to prove and protect your product/service's unique point of difference in a market place with very similar competitive products. You can start by going online and researching similar products on a national government patent/trademark website. You will save yourself a lot of time and money if you are able to see exactly what differences you need in order to patent or trademark an idea. If you don't have any patents or trademarks, you may benefit from legal advice to ensure that you are not infringing on your competition's trademarks and patents. You also need to have an idea of what it will cost in legal defense if your competition challenges you. The more you cut into the competitions market share, the greater the chances are that they will take action against you. Make sure your sales and marketing people are not infringing on competitors' trademarks without your knowledge in their marketing and advertising efforts. If your competition is bigger, more powerful and has the financial and legal ability to fight, they may put you out of business not only by imposing large legal fees, but also by attempting to interrupt your business and freeze your bank accounts. A large corporation may have a legal department or attorney on retainer that focuses on IP protection daily. A lot of people say that they don't want to pay legal fees; however, it is always advisable to have an expert's involvement to make sure all the "red tape" is handled and all the details are reviewed. In the long run, the precautions and preparations on the front end will be in place to protect you and keep you in compliance in an effort to avoid future problems.

15

IDENTIFYING THE PITFALLS BEFORE YOU STEP IN THE HOLE

"A plan saves time. Time saves money.
Money saves partnerships and relationships."

How you do anything is how you do everything. We are creatures of habit. Typically, the habits and care we give to details in one area of our lives is consistent with other areas of our lives. When there is a disconnection with this logic, there are usually signs of difficulty. If you are a detail person in how you handle your finances but not with your sales force, reevaluate the situation. Are there opportunity areas for improvement with your sales force that you have overlooked? Is a solution to hire someone who can pay attention to the details a viable and affordable option?

List three challenging areas in your business that you have managed differently from the usual way you manage activities that have been successful.

1. _____

2. _____

3. _____

Is there a correlation between the successful and challenging activities and your management approach or choices?

One of the interesting things about approaching this subject is that most everyone is quite willing to share what they have learned. And many times they may actually have a sense of humor while explaining the events, especially if they have overcome some hard times and moved forward to achieve success. Usually at the least, you will, get some emotion from them. True leaders have all had their challenges and their advice is invaluable. For example:

1. Think twice before you borrow capital from family and friends that can't afford to lose their investment or that you cannot afford to lose their friendship. Just because they are your family or friends doesn't mean they understand business. Choose your investors for their ability to objectively contribute to the growth of your business, not because you know them.

2. You may want to consider other options before hiring family and friends to do sales and marketing if they are not best-suited for the job. When considering an alliance or strategic partnership with a privately held company, notice if their sales and marketing people are all family members or if they are hired because of their expertise. If it is obvious that

the sales and marketing people are in their positions because of their relationships and not their expertise, this may be a sign of how other decisions are made in the company.

In sales and marketing, being able to respond to market changes and being innovative with new marketing ideas requires effective decision making. Ineffective family members running the company may be an indication of a pattern of ineffective decision making that may affect your financial and time investment. Although retraining is an option, time and resistance to training must be considered in the equation. Not everyone is an effective salesperson. Some salespeople are best on the phone. Others are best in the field. Some would rather die than to talk to a stranger. If they don't like to connect with people, they probably aren't going to be a good fit even if they are your smartest and most popular siblings!

3. Delay starting or acquiring a business in an industry that you haven't worked in until you have management level working knowledge of the business. You need to understand all the obstacles to your success before you sign on the dotted line. It starts with understanding who, what and how the competition impacts your business.

4. Reconsider your decision to partner or work with a company that doesn't have an implemented functional business plan in place. I have found that if you ask for their business plan in advance you may not see the true picture. In other words, if they don't have one and didn't need one to borrow money for

the business because their relatives were the contributors instead of a lending institution, they will probably go online, download a template document, fill in a few blanks and give it to you. It may be better to ask for it when you meet at their facility. If they don't have one in their office ready to show to you, then they haven't been using one. The time it takes to convince them to get a plan, help them create a plan and then implement a plan will be time that eats away at your capital instead of selling products. Time is money and you can't afford to do business with people that are functioning at a slower and lower pace and level than you are. It is best to find a partner that has more to offer faster. That will enable you to get products out on the street and money in the bank sooner.

Always know how many months of startup capital you need to survive until profits come in. This will tell you how long you can spend with partners who aren't up to speed. Even if they have a business plan, are they willing to implement it effectively and objectively in a timely manner that fits into your timetable for cash flow? Family owned and run businesses have the most difficult time with this process because many of their decisions are not based on business logic but on family needs. That type of decision making may not be in your best interest because time is money and you only have so much capital. Where and who are you going to spend it on?

5. Reconsider doing business with companies that have a messy office or facility, especially in the food and

beverage industry. Always try to meet them at their facility so you can see who is running the operation and how things are done. If you walk in and see disorganization, dirt, bugs, pets and unauthorized people wandering around in the office or production area, reconsider. Is this an example of how they run everything else? Details and first impressions are very important and if good business practices are not important to them, it is best to walk away.

The same theory applies in sales and marketing, details and first impressions are everything! Entrepreneurs like doing things their own way. One example is by having their pets in the work area. Unfortunately pets usually have fleas. The pet may stay in the designated area but the fleas do not. Pets can be totally inappropriate in healthcare and food and beverage processing facilities. In other industries, pets in the work place may be more acceptable. Nonetheless, liability in the event that a customer is bitten is another concern.

6. Reconsider working with family run businesses when the number of family households being supported is more than the number of family members actually working in the business effectively. When you go to their facility, try to meet all the family and close friends and ask about their kids and other relatives in a polite and social way. You will very quickly be able to determine just how much money is going out versus how much labor is going into the business.

7. Reconsider working internationally in a country that English is not the primary language unless you are fluent in that country's language and culture. You will never survive long term without key staff members that you can trust to interpret for you in many cultures. For example, although you may be fluent in Chinese, if you don't know the culture you won't last long.

8. Reconsider partnering with a company in a foreign county that you don't have key contact people in positions of authority located in that country with a vested interest in your success. Have a backup plan in the event that those in charge and your contact person lose their positioning, which negatively affects your business. It is best to identify and understand the added risks and variables that will be out of your control and have a plan of action in the event that you lose control.

Reconsider doing international business if you can't afford to lose your investment and/or pay to defend it in international courts. Business rules of play and honor don't always apply in other cultures. The deal may work the first two or three times, but if there's a scam it will usually come after you have become comfortable with your relationship, compensation, product deliveries and so forth. Then you get taken.

Always suspect that your products are being illegally duplicated. Your foreign partners will evaluate you and they will determine just how far you can afford to protect your products. None of these things may happen, but always be aware that they can. Remain vigilant at all times so you will see the signs if they do, or at least be able to maneuver with less "shell shock" than if you weren't able to see it coming.

Part of an effective business plan includes details on identifying when it's time to cut the losses and shut the door on your business if it's no longer profitable. Better yet, the time to sell your business is before you start to "hemorrhage" and profitability dramatically falls. For example, dominating market changes such as the attacks on September 11, 2001 immediately changed the course of many businesses as well as many lives. Some smart business owners had a plan for the worst-case scenario, therefore they knew immediately what to do. Others never thought it could happen and could have saved some of their assets if they had a business plan that addressed the "what if" situation. A plan saves time. Time saves money. Money saves partnerships and relationships.

List three experiences that you have had in your business as it relates to sales and marketing that you would not do again.

1. _____

2. _____

3. _____

Unless you are planning to create a timely, effective, and viable solution for a problem product or problem location; it may be better to find a better product or location. For example, a product with a questionable safety profile is still a questionable product even with a bigger warning label and more liability insurance. Sometimes things just aren't going to work, even if the product was your life's work creation. Resources are better spent on a different product.

List three examples of problem products or problem locations that you have experienced or observed that could have been effectively addressed differently in an effort to continue the profitability of the company.

1. _____

2. _____

3. _____

Have a clear picture of what a situation looks like when it's time to make a change in your business: when to walk, when to talk, when to borrow, when to grow, when to fire, when to hire and the most difficult is when to close the front door and move on. The interpretation of what a need for change looks like will be different for each person based on their personal tolerance, financial stability and experience level. Therefore, a clear picture is needed as to what your business continuance levels will be. Tolerating asset-depleting situations too long without making changes costs time and money and jeopardizes the future stability of the business. These can be the hardest decisions to make especially since they need to be made in a timely and accurate way.

It is best to be aware of the negative consequences that the inability to make timely business decisions has on your personal relationships and with the people who rely on your income and presence in their lives. An effective business plan with detailed trigger points with accountability for change should be in place and agreed upon by all of those who are vested in the outcome of the business' success. This includes an understanding by your family members that in order to continue the success of the business, certain sacrifices may be required if certain accountabilities are not reached. When the handwriting is on the wall, even the best chains stores and retailers know that they have to revamp their business plan to accommodate change and continue sustained growth. As mentioned in Chapter 14, we never go into business or start businesses thinking about a time to sell or close the doors. The truth is, though, that most successful business owners go into business aware that the true value of the business goes way beyond the day-to-day revenue that comes in. The true value of any company is its assets as it relates to net worth and how the next investor/buyer may view it. The goal for the successful small business owner is to build equity and value. The time to move on may be determined by when the next eager buyer with a vision appears in your office. Being free to pursue the next adventure could be more advantageous than you ever imagined. It's a matter of being brave enough to let go and move on.

16

THE LOOK OF SUCCESS

"We never lose any of our knowledge;
we carry it forward to our next adventure."

Now that you have learned how successful salespeople operate and what their mindset and tools for success are, you
are more prepared to continue on the incredible journey of
entrepreneurship. The main question, is will you regret not
trying to fulfill your dream of business ownership? Some
people have no desire at all to own their own business; they
love the security of working for someone else. But those
of you who understand the unexplainable desire to create
your own path make up the nearly 97% of all small business
owners in America. Small businesses are the heart and soul
of our country. You may feel alone but you are not. You
are surrounded by fellow creators. It's the American dream
and it starts with surrounding yourself with amazing team
members that get you excited. Celebrate your successes,
as small as they may seem, all along the way. It may seem

scary to learn things we don't know, but we have all been there. Most of the businesses we see today started because of dreams and vision. You can see and feel what has made this country great every time you drive down the street. The different store signs and advertisements should help you keep the vision of possibilities. Every morning and every evening before going to sleep, create and recall your vision of your business being exactly the way you want it to be and flowing the way you want it to flow. Always keep your goals and purpose in mind.

We are all unique people and we offer unique solutions to each situation. If we get stuck in our businesses and need answers, it is helpful to remember that really, all we need to know are the right questions, systems, or steps to follow. The answers may change over time, but usually the questions are the same. We can figure the rest out. We have a lifetime of experiences and we know a lot about a lot of things. We just need to know when to get help and what the help needs to look like. It's when you "don't know what you don't know" that the biggest challenge arises, but since you are reading this book, you have seen the merit in searching and being aware, which are the first steps in a lifetime of being a successful entrepreneur. The desire to keep learning, questioning and growing is never ending. Many times, the problems are small. It's just a process of realizing what is worth worrying about.

We never lose any of our knowledge; we carry it forward to our next adventure. I have found in my experience that our knowledge, growth and understanding of sales development, communication skills, industry knowledge etc. stays with us even if we have to close the doors. Many billionaires and great people in business have failed, but they kept their eye on the goal to recognize new opportunities. Our failures are the training ground and stepping stones for future successes.

Opportunities are all around you everywhere you look. There are hundreds of solutions to any one problem. Follow the guidelines of what has been successful in your industry and avoid the pitfalls of what hasn't been successful. Industry knowledge can be one of your greatest assets. If you can see it, you can believe it and then achieve it. Anything in your mind's eye is possible. Your future possibilities are endless. There is a reason why people like sales; it's because there is no cap on the potential success. The opportunities are endless!